CALENDARS
OF AMERICAN LITERARY
MANUSCRIPTS

THE LITERARY MANUSCRIPTS

OF HART CRANE

The Literary Manuscripts of Hart Crane is the first number in a series of CALENDARS OF AMERICAN LITERARY MANUSCRIPTS. Calendars of American Literary Manuscripts operates under the control of its Editorial Board on the advice of its Advisory Board. It is affiliated with the Ohio State Center for Textual Studies.

THE LITERARY MANUSCRIPTS OF

HART CRANE

COMPILED BY KENNETH A. LOHF

OHIO STATE UNIVERSITY PRESS

FOREWORD

One no longer has to justify the idea of systematically presenting knowledge gained from an intensive search for American literary manuscripts. The development of a criticism based on close and sophisticated reading of texts has increased the importance of allied scholarly arts for which that knowledge is essential; and the successes of the *National Union Catalog of Manuscript Collections* (Washington, D.C., 1959———) and *American Literary Manuscripts,* (Austin, 1960) have indicated the value of establishing the breadth of the available manuscript resources for the study of our national literature. There is some point, however, in introducing *Calendars of American Literary Manuscripts* because this project aims to contribute primary knowledge about American manuscripts in a depth greater than that attempted by those mentioned above.

The scholar's situation most often demands that he be able to locate a particular manuscript or family of manuscripts of a given literary work. Even a comprehensive list of bulk collections will indicate to him only the likely starting points for his quest. Since the manuscripts of most American authors are widely dispersed, that quest will most often involve wide correspondence and intensive research over an ever-increasing area. And, of course, one can rarely be satisfied that any discovery has terminated the hunt. To this point, almost every student who has had need of manuscript materials for an investigation in a field new to him has had to perform the quest afresh—even if, as is frequently true, the same quest had engaged others before him. It is an expensive, time-consuming, and often frustrating task; when it is performed redundantly, it is also shamefully wasteful of the resources of those in professions that can least afford waste.

Simply, *Calendars of American Literary Manuscripts* hopes to minimize this kind of waste by publishing the results of specialized searches for all of the available pre- and post-publication inscriptions of individual authors. With this kind of foundation, further explorations into the broad area we designate as manuscript materials should enlarge, rather than duplicate, information about the available. That is our major wish. We hope for subsidiary benefits as well: for an increase in the use of manuscript materials in scholarly and critical studies of American writers, for added impetus to research and criticism in American literature generally, and for the emergence of the incalculably large body of submerged American literary manuscripts.

One of the functions we have assumed grows out of the great difficulty in describing the always unique inscriptions of a writer trying out his art. The extreme variations in practice and materials resists the kind of codification possible for communicating information about printed states of a work. There probably will never be available to the manuscript user a language as precise as that of the bibliographer, but it should be possible to construct a reasonably applicable set of principles of vocabulary, treatment, and format for manuscript analyses. Those principles here, of course, must evolve out of the experiences of contributors to this series; the introduction to this volume records the principles we now submit for the consideration of those who will use them; future volumes in the series will attempt to progress further in the same delicate balance between the necessity for conventions and the requirements of the unique.

JOSEPH KATZ

Columbus, Ohio

PREFACE

To critics and scholars the perceptive use of an author's manuscripts and correspondence is of paramount and final importance. A close reading of these original documents, especially when they have survived in some measure of completeness, can reveal the author's sources, his methods of composition, the intuition and intellect that direct his imagination, and the biographical elements that influence his thought and action. Since Hart Crane's poetry is distinguished by a compact imagery and complex rhetoric, reminiscent of the French symbolists and the English metaphysicals, his work requires close study. Fortunately, a considerable corpus of the poet's manuscripts and letters available for such study is assured preservation in some sixteen repositories throughout the United States.

While not all of the early poems collected in *White Buildings* (New York, 1926) are known to exist in manuscript form, those poems published in *The Bridge* (New York, 1930) and those written after 1926 have nearly all survived, and many in several versions, to furnish a considerable record of the growth of a unique and powerful talent. Of one poem, the "Cape Hatteras" section from *The Bridge*, thirteen worksheets, drafts, and typescripts exist; and of another, "Voyages II," published in *White Buildings*, fifteen manuscripts are recorded. Four complete manuscripts of *The Bridge*, two of *White Buildings*, and two of "Key West," the collection on which the poet was working at the time of his suicide, are in institutional archives. This profusion is all the more remarkable when one considers Crane's short life (he died at the age of thirty-three), his essentially despairing nature, and the numerous places in which he lived and to which he traveled.

However, he sent his poems to his mother, Grace Hart Crane, to the editors of the literary reviews of the 1920's, and to his friends, notably Waldo Frank and Gorham Munson; and they, fortunately, preserved them in their files.

In the collections of the sixteen American libraries 278 manuscripts and 805 pieces of correspondence are held, as well as 455 letters written to Crane. The Hart Crane Collection at the Columbia University Libraries, the poet's own files, is the largest and most significant archive; and, in addition to the manuscripts described in the catalogue, it includes Crane's photographs, art work, and 141 volumes from his library. Also noteworthy are the collections at the libraries of the University of Chicago (Harriet Monroe Modern Poetry Collection), Fisk University (Jean Toomer Papers), the Ohio State University (Gorham Munson Papers), the University of Pennsylvania (Waldo Frank Papers), Princeton University (Otto Kahn and Allen Tate Papers), Southern Illinois University (Expatriate Collection), the University of Texas, and Yale University (*The Dial* Papers). Smaller groups of materials are housed at the University of Buffalo, Harvard University, Indiana University, the Library of Congress, the Newberry Library, Syracuse University, and the University of Virginia. Letters in private collections have been included when this information has been made available.

A survey of Crane manuscripts illustrates the wide dispersal, from New York to Texas, of the research materials for a single author, and it indicates, at least from the physical point of view, the difficulties attendant upon this phase of scholarship. One of the aims of this catalogue is to restore a unity to the extant Hart Crane manuscripts, thereby facilitating and contributing to the future critical and biographical investigations that this poet's work and life merit.

The bibliographical methodology for the description of printed materials has been widely applied and accepted. However, no such standards exist for the description of manuscripts, although the basic elements—citation, transcription, collation, dating, and enumeration—are essential in describing any literary work regardless of type. Consequently, in this compilation I have been guided by the unique physical properties of the manuscripts themselves and by their bibliographical relation to printed materials.

The manuscripts forming *White Buildings, The Bridge,* and "Key West" (Parts A, B, and C in the catalogue) have been grouped in the order in which they were published in book form, the complete manuscripts of the volumes in each part preceding the listing of individual poems that comprise the volumes. Minor, uncollected, and unpublished poems are listed alphabetically in Part D. The prose and other miscellaneous manuscripts enumerated in Part E are likewise listed alphabetically. Where more than one manuscript of an individual poem or prose work exists, they have been listed in chronological order in so far as this has been possible. In each part of the catalogue the entries have been numbered serially.

The following descriptive information is given for each manuscript:

Citation: Published title; type of manuscript, i.e., typewritten or autograph; pagination; notation concerning the handwriting or typing medium, i.e., ink, pencil, black ribbon, black carbon; and library location symbol.

Title: Transcription of the title as it appears on the manuscript, indicating capitalization, line endings, and underscoring (through use of italics).

First line: Transcription of the first line of a poem, or the first two lines in the case of brief lines.

Collation: Number of sheets; type of paper and color if other than white; size of paper in centimeters, height preceding width; numbering of sheets; and notes pertinent to the physical condition of the manuscript. Unless otherwise stated, it is understood that the manuscript is written or typed on the recto of the sheet only, the verso being blank.

Date: Specific or approximate date of composition. Since

most of the manuscripts are undated, the dating of individual pieces has been based either on internal evidence or on references in the Crane letters.

Contents: Identification of the class of the manuscript, i.e., draft, worksheet, notes, typescript; numbers of stanzas and lines; indication of publication only in cases where the specific draft has been published; description of other markings or notations on the manuscript; and remarks pertinent to the comprehension of the contents.

When one of the above categories is lacking from the description of a manuscript, this means either that the information is lacking or that it is not applicable. Because of the complexity of certain of the book-length manuscripts, I have had to depart from the usual format in describing them, but I have provided the information in an arrangement suitable to the individual manuscript.

The checklists of letters are contained in Parts F and G, the former listing letters from Crane, the latter letters to Crane. In both parts the letters, notes, post cards, and telegrams are arranged alphabetically by either recipient or sender. Letters to or from an individual in a single repository are grouped in one citation. For each letter or group listed the following information is given: number of pieces of correspondence; places from which the letters were written (if more than two places, the abbreviation "V.p." is used); dates of the letters (if more than two letters are listed, the inclusive years are given); and library symbol or name of private collector. There are two indexes to the catalogue: one to personal names and the titles of poems; the other, to repositories.

The making of any bibliography owes much to the efforts and help of others. I am particularly grateful to Brom Weber, of the University of California at Davis, for his investigations of the manuscripts as published in his *Hart Crane: A Biographical and Critical Study* (New York: The Bodley Press, 1948). His research has assisted my cataloguing, particularly when questions of date or the identification of fragments have been involved. I am also indebted to the librarians of the various Crane archives, who have generously reported their holdings and have provided reproductions for my use. In this regard, I am especially grateful to Alexander P. Clark, of the Princeton University Library; Donald C. Gallup, of the Beinecke Library at Yale University; Mary M. Hirth, of the Academic Center Library at the University of Texas; Janet Lowrey, of the Harriet Monroe Modern Poetry Library at the University of Chicago; Richard A. Ploch, of the Ohio State University Libraries; Jessie Carney Smith, of Fisk University Library; and Neda M. Westlake, of the University of Pennsylvania Library. I wish also to thank Gordon N. Ray, of the Guggenheim Foundation, and Norman Holmes Pearson, of Yale University, who have provided details concerning the letters in their collections.

Finally, I acknowledge the Columbia University Libraries' permission to reproduce the manuscripts appearing as illustrations in the catalogue.

KENNETH A. LOHF

Columbia University Libraries
March, 1967

CONTENTS

ILLUSTRATIONS

(Following page 76)

ABBREVIATIONS

References

BW   Brom Weber. *Hart Crane: A Biographical and Critical Study.* New York, The Bodley Press [1948]

CP   Hart Crane. *The Collected Poems of Hart Crane.* Edited with an introduction by Waldo Frank. New York, Liveright [1933]

LHC   Hart Crane. *The Letters of Hart Crane, 1916–1932.* Edited by Brom Weber. New York, Hermitage House [1952]

SL   Hart Crane. *Seven Lyrics.* Preface by Kenneth A. Lohf. [Cambridge, Mass.] The Ibex Press [1966]

TB   Hart Crane. *The Bridge.* New York, Liveright [1930]

WB   Hart Crane. *White Buildings.* [New York] Boni & Liveright, 1926.

Manuscript Abbreviations

a.l.s.   Autograph letter signed

a.ms.   Autograph manuscript

a.n.s.   Autograph note signed

n.d.   No date

n.y.   No year

p.c.s.   Post card signed

t.l.s.   Typewritten letter signed

t.ms.   Typewritten manuscript

t.n.   Typewritten note

v.p.   Various places

Library Symbols

CtY	Yale University, New Haven
DLC	Library of Congress, Washington
ICN	Newberry Library, Chicago
ICU	University of Chicago, Chicago
ICarbS	Southern Illinois University, Carbondale
InU	Indiana University, Bloomington
MH	Harvard University, Cambridge
NjP	Princeton University, Princeton
NBuU	University of Buffalo, Buffalo
NNC	Columbia University, New York
NSyU	Syracuse University, Syracuse
OU	Ohio State University, Columbus
PU	University of Pennsylvania, Philadelphia
TNF	Fisk University, Nashville
TxU	University of Texas, Austin
ViU	University of Virginia, Charlottesville

A.

WHITE BUILDINGS

Complete Manuscripts

A1. *White Buildings*: Notebook. T.ms., 134p. (black ribbon). NNC

Title: Hart's copies of his Poems [on p. 1, in pencil, probably Grace Hart Crane's hand]

Collation: 67 sheets of notebook paper with 3 punched holes along left margin. 21.4 x 13.7 cm. In an "McM No. K 010 Price Book" (three-ring binder), with black leatherette covers. Rectos numbered in pencil from 1 through 33; versos unnumbered but included in pagination.

Date: ca. 1917–1926. (Some poems individually dated.)

Contents: Typescripts of Crane's poems written up to time WB, his first volume, was published in 1926. Manuscripts in notebook not included in WB are "At Heaven Gates", "Belle Isle", "America's Plutonic Ecstacies", "Interior", "Legende", "To Portapovitch", "Porphyro in Akron", "Three Locutions Des Pierrots", "Interludium", "The Great Western Plains", "A Persuasion", "Postscript", and "Forgetfulness". Contents: 1. Title; 2–4. blank; 5. "Recitative". (Early version in 4 stanzas of 4 lines each); 6. blank; 7, 9, 11, 13, 15, 17. "Three Poems | For the Marriage of Faustus & Helen". ("Cleveland, 1923", typed on p. 17 at end of text); 8, 10, 12, 14, 16. blank; 19. "Possessions"; 20. blank; 21. "Voyages I". (Earlier typed title, "Poem", canceled and new title written in pencil, Crane's hand); 22. blank; 23. "Voyages II". (One correction in last line, and on bottom of page, "12/20/24", Crane's hand in pencil); 24. blank; 25.

"Voyages". (Title and first 2 lines of "Voyages III",
canceled in pencil); 26. "Voyages III"; 27. "Voyages
IV". (Typed lower right, "April - 24 | to EO"); 28.
blank; 29. "Legend". (Typed lower left, "Oct. '24");
30. blank; 31. "Stark Major". (Typed lower right, "Cleve-
land '23 | February"); 32. blank; 33. "My Grand-
mother's Love Letters"; 34. blank; 35. "At Heaven
Gates". (Typed lower right, "10/19/24". Unpublished
poem, 4 stanzas of 3, 5, 7, and 4 lines, respectively); 36.
"Feb. 21st '24 | Eugene O'Neill's | Ridgefield, Conn."
(Crane's hand in pencil, canceled in ink); 37. "Praise For
An Urn". (Typed lower right, "2/22"); 38. blank; 39.
"Garden Abstract"; 40. blank; 41. "Belle Isle". (Typed
lower right, "March, '23". Version as published in BW,
p. 391. Poem later revised to form "Voyages VI"); 42.
blank; 43. "Belle Isle". (Typed lower right, "2nd version"); 44. "He took hell all over himself" (Crane's
hand in pencil"); 45. "Pastorale". (Typed along left
margin, "July '21"); 46. blank; 47. "Paraphrase". (Typed
lower left, "Oct. '24"); 48. blank; 49. "Sunday Morning
Apples"; 50. blank; 51. "Chaplinesque". (Typed upper
left, "10/21"); 52. blank; 53. "Black Tambourine".
(Typed upper left, "3/21"); 54. blank; 55. "America's
Plutonic Ecstasies"; 56. blank; 57. "Interior"; 58. blank;
59. "Legende"; 60. blank; 61. "North Labrador" 62.
blank; 63. "To Portapovitch'; 64. blank; 65. "In Shadow";
66–68. blank; 69. "The Fernery"; 70. blank; 71, 73, 75.
"Porphyro in Akron"; 72, 74, 76. blank; 77–78. "Three |
Locutions Des Pierrots"; 79. "Interludium"; 80. blank;
81. "The Great Western Plains"; 82. blank; 83. "Lachrimae Christi". (Title, Crane's hand in pencil. Text contains 10 lines related to opening portions of "Cape
Hatteras" and not to title poem); 84–86. blank; 87. "A
Persuasion". (Typed upper left, "5/21"); 88. blank; 89.
"Postscript"; 90. blank; 91. "Forgetfulness"; 92. blank; 93.
"Table". (List of poems and places of publication); 94–
98. blank; 99. Notes concerning editions of Petronius

and Apuleius (Crane's hand in ink), and list of four titles for poems; 100–114. blank; 115–121, 123–126 (122 blank). Typescript copies of poems by Donne, Lope de Vega, Catullus, Pound, John Webster, Shakespeare, Coleridge, Campion, Raleigh, Landor, and Max Michelson; 127, 129, 131. "For the Marriage of Faustus & Helen". Part I complete and first 33 lines of Part III; 128, 130, 132. blank; 133. "Sam. | Julia Laverty | 78 Col. HS." (Crane's hand in pencil); 134. blank.

A2. *White Buildings.* T.ms., 40p. (black ribbon). NNC

Title: WHITE | BUILDINGS | by | HART CRANE | With A Foreword | by | Eugene O'Neill [canceled and "Allen Tate" written beneath, Crane's hand in pencil] | Ce ne peut être que la fin du monde, en avançant. | RIMBAUD

Collation: 40 sheets of typing paper. 32.8 x 21.5 cm. Two holes pierced at top of each sheet. Sheets unnumbered.

Date: ca. June 1926. (Probably manuscript referred to in letter from Crane to Waldo Frank, 19 June 1926. See LHC, pp. 258–59.)

Contents: Typescript of WB in which texts and sequence of poems are identical to those of volume published in 1926. Preliminary sheets are as follows: Cover title; Title page; Foreword (no text); Acknowledgments page; Contents page. Final sheet of manuscript blank. Unsigned note on cover title in ink to Waldo Frank, in which Crane writes that manuscript is "exactly as you saw on the Isle of Pines—and as submitted finally for publication." Emendations on title-page, acknowledgments page, and contents page (Crane's hand in pencil). One correction in pencil (Crane's hand) on sheet containing "Voyages III". On the verso of final sheet (Crane's hand in ink), "á seis hora hoy Cafe la Diana" and several additional words in Spanish.

Individual Poems

A3.   "Black Tambourine". T.ms., 1p. (black ribbon). OU
Title: BLACK TAMBORINE
First line: The interests of a black man in a cellar
Collation: 1 sheet of typing paper. 28.3 x 21.5 cm. (Enclosed in letter from Crane to Gorham B. Munson, 24 February [1921].)
Date: 24 February 1921.
Contents: Early typescript, 3 stanzas of 4 lines each, as published in BW, pp. 95–96.

A4.   "Black Tambourine". A.ms., 1p. (Crane's hand in pencil). ICarbS
Title: Black Tamborine [Crane's hand in pencil]
First line: The interests of a black man in a cellar
Collation: 1 sheet of typing paper. 26.5 x 21.5 cm.
Date: ca. Spring 1921.
Contents: Early autograph draft, 3 stanzas of 4 lines each, differing from version published in BW, pp. 95–96. Pencil line drawn beneath last line of text.

A5.   "Black Tambourine; A Persuasion". T.ms., 1p. (black ribbon). CtY
Titles: BLACK TAMBOURINE; A PERSUASION
First lines: The interests of a black man in a cellar; If she waits late at night
Collation: 1 sheet of typing paper. 28 x 21.5 cm.

Date: ca. May 1921.

Contents: Typescripts of two poems on single sheet, "Black Tambourine" preceding "A Persuasion". Text of former is that published in WB, and of latter that published in BW, pp. 387–88.

A6. "Emblems of Conduct". T.ms., 1p. (black ribbon). OU

Title: *EMBLEMS OF CONDUCT*

First line: By a peninsula the painter sat and sketched

Collation: 1 sheet of tan typing paper. 27.8 x 20.5 cm.

Date: ca. 1920.

Contents: Early typescript draft, 3 stanzas of 6, 5, and 6 lines, respectively, differing from version published in WB.

A7. "My Grandmother's Love Letters". A.ms., 1p. (Crane's hand in ink). NNC

First lines: And I ask myself, | "Are your fingers long enough to play | old instruments?

Collation: 1 sheet of typing paper. 28 x 21.5 cm.

Date: ca. November 1919.

Contents: Early draft of second half of poem, 24 lines in 3 stanzas; corrections and emendations (Crane's hand in ink).

A8. "My Grandmother's Love Letters". T.ms., 1p. (black ribbon). NNC

Title: MY GRANDMOTHER'S LOVE LETTERS

First line: There are no stars tonight

Collation: 1 sheet of typing paper. 27.8 x 21.7 cm.

Date: ca. November 1919.

Contents: Typescript draft, 29 lines in 7 stanzas. Stanza 6 canceled in pencil and omitted from published versions. Typed lower right, "Hart Crane".

A9.   "My Grandmother's Love Letters". T.ms., 1p. (black carbon). NNC

Title: MY GRANDMOTHER'S LOVE LETTERS

First line: There are no stars tonight

Collation: 1 sheet of typing paper. 27.5 x 21.3 cm.

Date: ca. November 1919.

Contents: Typescript as published in *The Dial* and WB. One correction in pencil (probably Crane's hand).

A10.   "Praise for an Urn". T.ms., 1p. (black ribbon). MH

Title: *PRAISE FOR AN URN*

First line: It was a kind and northern face

Collation: 1 sheet of typing paper. 27.3 x 21 cm. (Enclosed in letter from Crane to William Stanley Braithwaite, 27 October 1922.)

Date: ca. June 1922.

Contents: Typescript, 6 stanzas of 4 lines each, as published in 1922 volume of *Anthology of Magazine Verse*, edited by W. S. Braithwaite. Typed lower right, "by Hart Crane | published in the Dial, June, '22".

A11.   "Garden Abstract". T.ms., 1p. (black ribbon). OU

Title: GARDEN ABSTRACT

First lines: The apple on its bough | Is my desire,—

Collation: 1 sheet of typing paper. 28 x 21.5 cm. (Enclosed in letter from Crane to Gorham B. Munson, 1 April [1920].)

Date: 1 April 1920.

Contents: Early typescript draft, 3 stanzas of 4, 6, and 5 lines, respectively, as published in BW, p. 76.

A12. "Stark Major". T.ms., 1p. (black ribbon). PU

Title: *STARK MAJOR*

First line: The lover's death—how regular

Collation: 1 sheet of typing paper. 28 x 21.5 cm.

Date: ca. January-February 1923.

Contents: Typescript, 6 stanzas of 4 lines each. Typed lower right, "Hart Crane".

A13. "Chaplinesque". T.ms., 1p. (black ribbon). OU

Title: Chaplinesque [supplied in text of letter]

First line: Contented with such random consolations

Collation: 1 sheet of typing paper. 28 x 21.5 cm. (On first page of letter from Crane to Gorham B. Munson, 1 October 1921.)

Date: 1 October 1921.

Contents: Early typescript draft of lines which form first 3 stanzas of final version, 2 stanzas of 8 and 6 lines, as published in BW, pp. 108–9.

A14. "Chaplinesque". T.ms., 1p. (black ribbon). OU

Title: CHAPLINESQUE | [double rule] | To Charles Chaplin

First line: We make our meek adjustments

Collation: 1 sheet of typing paper. 25.5 x 21.5 cm. (On verso of letter from Crane to Gorham B. Munson, 6 October, 1921.)

Date: 6 October 1921.

Contents: Late typescript varying in several instances from version published in WB.

A15. "Possessions". T.ms., 1p. (black ribbon). TNF

Title: POSSESSIONS

First line: Witness now this trust! the rain

Collation: 1 sheet of typing paper. 27.8 x 21.5 cm.

Date: ca. Autumn 1923.

Contents: Typescript draft which most nearly corresponds to one published in *The Little Review* (Spring 1924), with several variations, and differing from version which appeared in WB.

A16. "Lachrymae Christi". T.ms., 1p. (black ribbon). TNF

Title: LACHRIMAE CHRISTI

First lines: Recall to music | and set down at last

Collation: 1 sheet of typing paper. 27.8 x 21.5 cm.

Date: ca. February 1924.

Contents: Early typescript draft, 26 lines in 6 stanzas of varying lengths, as published in BW, pp. 225–26.

A17. "Lachrymae Christi". T.ms., 1p. (black ribbon). PU

Title: LACHRYMAE CHRISTI

First line: Recall to music and set down at last

Collation: 1 sheet of typing paper. 28 x 21.5 cm.

Date: ca. February 1924.

Contents: Early typescript draft, 20 lines in 4 stanzas of varying lengths, as published in BW, pp. 226–27.

A18. "Lachrymae Christi". T.ms., 1p. (black carbon). PU

Title: LACHRYMAE CHRISTI

First line: These pyramids of nights

Collation: 1 sheet of typing paper. 28 x 21.5 cm.

Date: 3 March 1925.

Contents: Typescript draft, 29 lines in 8 stanzas of varying lengths, differing from versions published in WB and BW. Lower right, Crane's hand in ink, "3/3/25 | A new version— | But I hope—better. | Love, Waldo— | Hart".

A19. "Passage". T.ms., 1p. (black ribbon). PU

Title: *PASSAGE*

First line: Where the cedar leaf divides the sky

Collation: 1 sheet of typing paper. 28 x 21.5 cm.

Date: ca. June 1925.

Contents: Typescript, 37 lines in 7 stanzas of varying lengths, as published in *The Calendar* (July 1926) and WB. Typed lower right, "by Hart Crane".

A20. "The Wine Menagerie". T.ms., 2p. (black ribbon). TxU

Title: THE WINE MENAGERIE

First line: Invariable when wine redeems the sight,

Collation: 2 sheets of typing paper. 28 x 21.5 cm. Second sheet numbered 2.

Date: ca. October 1925.

Contents: Typescript, 11 stanzas of varying lengths, as published in WB, with minor variations.

A21. "Recitative". T.ms., 1p. (black ribbon). TNF

Title: *RECITATIVE*

First line: Look at me here, O Janus-faced . . .

Collation: 1 sheet of typing paper. 27.8 x 21.5 cm.

Date: ca. October 1923.

Contents: Early typescript draft, 4 stanzas of 4 lines each, varying from version published in BW, p. 224.

A22. "Recitative". T.ms., 1p. (black ribbon). OU

Title: RECITATIVE

First line: Regard the capture here, O Janus-faced—

Collation: 1 sheet of typing paper. 27.8 x 21.5 cm. (Enclosed in letter from Crane to Gorham B. Munson, 10 December 1923.)

Date: 10 December 1923.

Contents: Early typescript draft, 4 stanzas of 4 lines each, as published in BW, p. 224.

A23. "For the Marriage of Faustus and Helen". T.ms., 5p. (black ribbon). TxU

Title: *FOR THE MARRIAGE OF FAUSTUS AND HELEN*

First line: The mind has shown itself at times

Collation: 5 sheets of typing paper. 28 x 21.5 cm. Sheets unnumbered.

Date: ca. Winter-Spring 1923.

Contents: Typescript as published in *Broom* (January 1923). Inscription to Slater Brown on last sheet following text (Crane's hand in ink).

A24. "For the Marriage of Faustus and Helen". T.ms., 5p. (black carbon). CtY

Title: *FOR THE MARRIAGE OF FAUSTUS AND HELEN*

First line: The mind has shown itself at times

Collation: 5 sheets of typing paper. 27.8 x 21.5 cm. Last four sheets numbered 2 through 5 (Waldo Frank's hand), and numbered 6 through 10 (unknown hand). (Enclosed in letter from Crane to Alfred Stieglitz, 23 April 1923.)

Date: 23 April 1923.

Contents: Typescript as published in *Broom* (January 1923). Upper right on first sheet, "Postmark 1923 Apr 23" (Waldo Frank's hand). Signed inscription to Alfred Stieglitz on p. 5 following text (Crane's hand in ink).

A25. "For the Marriage of Faustus and Helen". T.ms., 5p. (black carbon). TNF

Title: *FOR THE MARRIAGE OF FAUS-TUS & HELEN*

First line: The mind has shown itself at times

Collation: 5 sheets of typing paper. 27.8 x 21.5 cm. Last four sheets numbered 2 through 5.

Date: ca. Winter-Spring 1923.

Contents: Typescript as published in *Broom* (January 1923). Typed on p. 5 following text, "by Hart Crane, 45 Grove St., | New York City".

A26. "For the Marriage of Faustus and Helen". T.ms., 1p. (black ribbon). NNC

First line: Religious gunman! that died too soon

Collation: 1 sheet of typing paper. 27.7 x 21.5 cm.

Date: ca. May 1922.

Contents: Early draft, 41 lines in 6 stanzas of varying lengths; corrections and emendations (Crane's hand in pencil).

A27. "For the Marriage of Faustus and Helen". T.ms., 2p. (black ribbon). OU

Title: THREE POEMS | FOR THE MARRIAGE OF FAUSTUS AND HELEN

First line: The mind has shown itself at times

Collation: 2 sheets of typing paper. 27.8 x 21.5 cm. Sheets unnumbered. (Enclosed in letter from Crane to Gorham B. Munson, 7 August 1922.)

Date: 7 August 1922.

Contents: Typescript of Part I in 7 stanzas, omitting seventh stanza of published version.

A28. "For the Marriage of Faustus and Helen". T.ms., 1p. (black ribbon). OU

First line: The earth may glide diaphanous to death

Collation: 1 sheet of typing paper. 27.8 x 21.5 cm. (Enclosed in letter from Crane to Gorham B. Munson, 29 September 1922.)

Date: 29 September 1922.

Contents: Typescript of seventh stanza of Part I.

A29. "For the Marriage of Faustus and Helen". T.ms., 1p. (black ribbon). OU

First line: Their windows staring intermittent testimony

Collation: 1 sheet of typing paper. 26 x 21 cm. (On verso of letter from Crane to Gorham B. Munson, ca. 1922, and incorporated into text.)

Date: ca. 1922.

Contents: Early typescript draft of Part III, stanza 3, 9 lines.

A30. "At Melville's Tomb". T.ms., 1p. (black ribbon). PU

Title: *AT MELVILLE'S TOMB*

First line: How many times the jewelled dice spoke

Collation: 1 sheet of typing paper. 28 x 21.5 cm. (On top half of sheet containing typewritten letter from Crane to Waldo Frank, 26 October [1925].)

Date: 26 October 1925.

Contents: Early typescript draft, 3 stanzas of 4 lines each.

A31. "Voyages I–VI". T.ms., 6p. (black carbon). NNC

Title: VOYAGES

Collation: 6 sheets of light-green typing paper. 27.8 x 21.2 cm. Sheets unnumbered. Two holes pierced along top with metal fasteners.

Date: ca. 1925.

Contents: Typescript of sequence of six poems as published in *The Little Review* (Spring-Summer 1926) and WB. "Hart's Ms." written on top of first sheet in pencil (probably Grace Hart Crane's hand).

A31a. "Voyages I". T.ms., 1p. (black ribbon). OU

Title: THE BOTTOM OF THE SEA IS CRUEL

First line: Above the fresh ruffles of the surf

Collation: 1 sheet of typing paper. 28 x 21.5 cm. (On second page of letter from Crane to Gorham B. Munson, 1 October 1921.)

Date: 1 October 1921.

Contents: Early typescript draft, 3 stanzas of 5, 4, and 6 lines, respectively, of poem which later became "Voyages I". This version differs from those published in *Secession* and WB.

A32. "Voyages II". T.ms., 2p. (black ribbon). NNC

Title: Notes for | V O Y A G E S

First line: That night off San Salvador

Collation: 1 sheet of tan typing paper, written on both sides. 27.7 x 21.5 cm. Two holes pierced along top of sheet.

Date: 27 September 1924.

Contents: On recto, early typewritten notes and drafts, dated lower right, "9/27/24"; two words (Crane's hand in pencil). On verso, three later drafts of stanza 1 and one draft of 3 lines from stanza 2.

A33. "Voyages II". T. and a.ms., 2p. (black ribbon; Crane's hand in pencil). NNC

Title: Voyages II [Crane's hand in pencil]

First line: The emulating tides that stride

Collation: 1 sheet of tan typing paper, written on both sides. 27.7 x 21.5 cm. Two holes pierced at top of sheet.

Date: ca. Autumn 1924.

Contents: On recto, early typescript draft of stanza 1 with emendations (Crane's hand in pencil); and early draft of stanza 2 at bottom of sheet (Crane's hand in pencil). On verso, typescript drafts of stanza 5 with notes in pencil (Crane's hand) at the bottom of the sheet.

A34. "Voyages II'. T. and a.ms., 1p. (black ribbon; Crane's hand in pencil). NNC

First lines: vermiculate | aureate | Take this sea, then, veined and processioned,

Collation: 1 sheet of typing paper. 27.5 x 21.3 cm. Two holes pierced at top of sheet.

Date: ca. Autumn 1924.

Contents: Drafts of stanza 2, 16 typewritten lines and 12 lines (Crane's hand in pencil).

A35. "Voyages II". T.ms., 2p. (black ribbon). NNC

Title: *Voyages II*

First line: —And yet this great wink of eternity,

Collation: 1 sheet of typing paper, written on both sides. 27.8 x 21.5 cm. Two holes pierced at top of sheet.

Date: ca. Autumn 1924.

Contents: On recto, two late typescript drafts of first two stanzas, last 2 lines in pencil (Crane's hand). On verso, two late typescript drafts of first three stanzas; emendations (Crane's hand in pencil).

A36. "Voyages II". T. and a.ms., 2p. (black ribbon; Crane's hand in ink). NNC

Title: *Voyages II*

First line: —And yet this great wink of eternity,

Collation: 1 sheet of typing paper, written on both sides. 27.8 x 21.5 cm. Two holes pierced at top and bottom of sheet.

Date: ca. Autumn 1924.

Contents: On recto, late typescript drafts of first two stanzas, 9 lines typewritten and last line in pencil (Crane's hand). On verso, drafts of portions of stanzas 3 and 5, 6 lines (Crane's hand in ink) and 4 typewritten lines.

A37. "Voyages II". T.ms., 1p. (black ribbon). NNC

Title: VOYAGES – II [typed beneath 6 lines canceled in pencil]

First line: Frondage of dark islands, breathing

Collation: 1 sheet of typing paper. 27.5 x 21.3 cm. Two holes pierced at top of sheet

Date: ca. Autumn 1924.

Contents: Drafts of stanza 3, 22 typewritten lines and 5 lines in pencil; emendations and corrections (Crane's hand in pencil). (See Fig. 1.)

A38. "Voyages II". T.ms., 2p. (black ribbon). NNC

Title: Announce [Crane's hand in pencil]

First line: Frondage of dark islands, breathing

Collation: 1 sheet of tan typing paper, written on both sides. 27.8 x 21.5 cm. Two holes pierced at top of sheet.

Date: ca. Autumn 1924.

Contents: On recto, drafts of stanza 3, 23 typewritten lines and 2 lines in pencil; corrections and emendations (Crane's hand in pencil). On verso, draft of 3 lines from stanza 5 (Crane's hand in pencil) canceled in pencil; and on bottom of sheet, 15-word signed note to a Mrs. Keene (Crane's hand in pencil).

A39. "Voyages II". T.ms., 2p. (black ribbon). NNC
Title: V O Y A G E S II
First line: Frondage of dark islands, breathing
Collation: 1 sheet of typing paper, written on both sides. 27.5 x 21.3 cm. Two holes pierced at top of sheet.
Date: ca. Autumn 1924.
Contents: On recto, drafts of stanza 3, 24 typewritten lines, with emendations (Crane's hand in pencil). On verso, drafts of stanza 5, 28 typewritten lines, with three emendations (Crane's hand in pencil).

A40. "Voyages II". T. and a.ms., 1p. (black ribbon; Crane's hand in pencil). NNC
First line: —And yet this great wink of eternity
Collation: 1 sheet of tan typing paper. 27.7 x 21.5 cm. Two holes pierced at top of sheet. Lower right corner of sheet torn away.
Date: ca. Autmun 1924.
Contents: Typescript draft of first 3 stanzas, with 4 lines in pencil at bottom of sheet. Upper left, "adagio" (Crane's hand in pencil).

A41. "Voyages II". T. and a.ms., 2p. (black ribbon; Crane's hand in pencil). NNC
First line: —And yet this great wink of eternity
Collation: 1 sheet of tan typing paper, written on both sides. 27.7 x 21.5 cm. Two holes pierced at top of sheet.
Date: ca. Autumn 1924.

Contents: On recto, drafts of first 3 stanzas, 16 type-written lines, and 7 lines in pencil from stanza 3. On verso, drafts of stanzas 4 and 1 (Crane's hand in pencil).

A42. "Voyages II". T. and a.ms., 2p. (black ribbon; Crane's hand in pencil). NNC

First line: —And yet this great wink of eternity

Collation: 1 sheet of tan typing paper, written on both sides. 27.7 x 21.5 cm. Two holes pierced at top of sheet.

Date: ca. Autumn 1924.

Contents: On recto, draft of first 3 stanzas, 10 type-written lines, and 5 lines in pencil from stanza 3. On verso, typescript draft of stanza 3, 6 lines; and draft in pencil, (Crane's hand) of unpublished poem, "To Bhudda", 4 lines.

A43. "Voyages II". T. and a.ms., 1p. (black ribbon; Crane's hand in pencil). NNC

Title: *Voyages II*

First line: —And yet this great wink of eternity,

Collation: 1 sheet of typing paper. 27.8 x 21.5 cm. Two holes pierced at top of sheet.

Date: ca. Autumn 1924.

Contents: Late drafts of first 3 stanzas, first 2 stanzas typewritten, and stanza 3 (Crane's hand in pencil).

A44. "Voyages II". T. and a.ms., 2p. (black ribbon; Crane's hand in pencil). NNC

Title: Voyages II [Crane's hand in pencil]

First line: Frondage of dark islands, breathing

Collation: 1 sheet of tan typing paper, written on both sides. 27.7 x 21.5 cm. Two holes pierced at top of sheet.

Date: ca. Autumn 1924.

Contents: On recto, early typescript draft of poem in 4 stanzas; corrections and emendations (Crane's hand in pencil). On verso, miscellaneous notes and drafts (Crane's hand in pencil).

A45. "Voyages II". T.ms., 1p. (black ribbon). CtY
Title: *Voyages II*
First line: —And yet this great wink of eternity,
Collation: 1 sheet of typing paper. 27.8 x 21.5 cm.
Date: ca. December 1924.
Contents: Late typescript, 5 stanzas of 5 lines each.

A46. "Voyages II". T.ms., 1p. (black ribbon). PU
Title: *V O Y A G E S | 2*
First line: —And yet this great wink of eternity,
Collation: 1 sheet of typing paper. 28 x 21.5 cm.
Date: 3 January 1925.
Contents: Late typescript draft, 5 stanzas of 5 lines each. Lower right, inscription in ink to Waldo Frank, signed and dated 3 January 1925.

A47. "Voyages III". T.ms., 1p. (black ribbon). PU
Title: *VOYAGES*
First line: Infinite consanguinity it bears—
Collation: 1 sheet of typing paper. 28 x 21.5 cm.
Date: ca. Autumn 1924.
Contents: Late typescript, 19 lines in 4 stanzas of varying lengths. Lower right, undated typewritten note to Waldo Frank. Earlier version of "Voyages III" is sonnet "What

miles I gather up and unto you" (see items D101 and D102).

A48. "Voyages III". T.ms., 1p. (black ribbon). TxU

Title: *VOYAGES*

First line: Infinite consanguinity it bears—

Collation: 1 sheet of typing paper. 28 x 21.5 cm.

Date: ca. Autumn 1924.

Contents: Late typescript, 19 lines in 4 stanzas of varying lengths. Typed lower right, "by Hart Crane, | 110 Columbia Heights, | Brooklyn, N.Y."

A49. "Voyages IV". T.ms., 1p. (black ribbon). TNF

Title: V O Y A G E S

First line: Whose counted smile of hours and days, suppose

Collation: 1 sheet of typing paper. 27.5 x 21.5 cm.

Date: ca. Summer 1924.

Contents: Early typescript draft, 24 lines in 6 stanzas of varying lengths.

A50. "Voyages IV". T.ms., 1p. (black ribbon). PU

Title: VOYAGES

First line: Whose counted smile of hours and days, suppose

Collation: 1 sheet of typing paper. 28 x 21.5 cm. (Typed on top two-thirds of sheet containing letter from Crane to Waldo Frank, 6 September 1924.)

Date: 6 September 1924.

Contents: Early typescript draft, 25 lines in 5 stanzas of varying lengths.

A51. "Voyages VI". T.ms., 1p. (black ribbon). TxU

Title: V O Y A G E S | VI

First line: Where icy and bright dungeons lift

Collation: 1 sheet of typing paper. 28 x 21.5 cm.

Date: ca. 1925.

Contents: Early typescript, 5 stanzas of 4 lines each, differing from version published in WB. Earlier version of "Voyages VI" is poem "Belle Isle" (see item D7).

B.

THE BRIDGE

B1. *The Bridge*. T.ms., 3 preliminary pages, pp. 2–19, 21–43 (black carbon; title-page and note on p. 39, black ribbon). NNC

Title: *THE* | *BRIDGE* | A POEM | by HART CRANE | [epigraph from The Book of Job on three lines]

Collation: 44 sheets of typing paper. 27.8 x 21.5 cm. Preliminary sheets unnumbered, other sheets numbered 2–19, 21–43; pp. 1 and 20 lacking.

Date: ca. 1928. (Probably copy of version sent by Crane to Otto Kahn in late 1928 or early 1929.)

Contents: Title-page; Acknowledgements page; Contents page; [Dedication: To Brooklyn Bridge] p. 2 (final 4 stanzas only); I. "Ave Maria", pp 3–6; II. "Powhatan's Daughter", pp. 7–19 ("The Harbor Dawn" pp. 8–9, "Van Winkle" pp. 10–11, "The River" pp. 12–15, "The Dance" pp. 16–19); III. "Cutty Sark", pp. 21–24; IV. "Cape Hatteras", p. 25 (title-page only, text lacking); V. "Three Songs", pp. 26–30 ("Southern Cross" pp. 27–28, "National Winter Garden" p. 29, "Virginia" p. 30); VI. "The Cyder Cask", p. 31 (title-page only, text lacking); VII. "The Calgary Express", p. 32 (title-page only, text lacking); VIII. "1927 Whistles", p. 33 (title-page only, text lacking); IX. "The Tunnel", pp. 34–38; X. "Atlantis", pp. 39–43. Minor corrections in ink on pp. 8, 10, 15, 18, 35, and 41, Crane's hand.

Note: NNC also has negative photostats of typescript of *The Bridge* which was given to Peter Blume and which is identical with copy described here. Photostats include only following pages: Contents page, pp-4–5, 10–11, 27, 30, 32–33 (with second photostat of p. 32 bearing corrections by Crane), 40–43, and five pages of "Cape Hatteras" separately paged.

B2.　*The Bridge.* T.ms., various pagings (black ribbon and black carbon). NNC

Title: *THE | BRIDGE |* A POEM | by HART CRANE | With a Frontispiece from | the painting of Brooklyn Bridge | by Joseph Stella | [epigraph from The Book of Job on three lines] | Editions Narcisse | (etc)

Date: ca. April-September 1929. Final poem, "Atlantis", dated "Paris—July 14th '29" (Crane's hand). Revised version of "Cutty Sark" annotated by Caresse Crosby "rec'd Sept 14", and "final version" of "Cape Hatteras" signed and dated "9/17/29" (Crane's hand) and annotated "rec'd Sept 30" by Caresse Crosby. From letters of Caresse Crosby to Crane in collection at NNC we know that the Crosbys read a manuscript as early as April 29, began to set it in proof by August 6, and mailed review copies on February 11, 1930.

Contents: Manuscript of "The Bridge" as received by Harry and Caresse Crosby at the Black Sun Press in Paris and published by them in January 1930. Contents:

a. Preliminary sheets: Title-page, half-title page, dedication page, and contents page. T.ms., 4p. (black ribbon). 4 sheets of white stationery. 18 x 14 cm. Sheets numbered 1 through 4 in red pencil, lower left. Notations in ink and pencil (Crane's hand).

b. "To Brooklyn Bridge". T.ms., 2 p. (black ribbon). 1 sheet of white stationery, written on both sides. 18 x 14 cm. On recto, lower left, sheet numbered 5 in red pencil, and top left, numbered 1 in pencil; on verso, top left, sheet numbered 2 in pencil. Notation and emendation (Crane's hand in ink).

c. "I | Ave Maria". T.ms., 4p. (black ribbon and black carbon). 4 sheets of typing paper. 21 x 16.2 cm. Sheets numbered 3 through 6 in pencil, upper left, and numbered 6 through 9 in red pencil, lower right. Page 4 (numbered in pencil) is black ribbon, other pages black carbon. Notations in ink (Crane's hand). Pinned to p. 4, upper right, is gloss to first stanza, typed on light-blue piece of typing paper, 8 x 21 cm.

d. "I | Ave Maria". T.ms., 4p. (black ribbon and black carbon). 4 sheets of typing paper. 21 x 16.2 cm. Last two sheets numbered 2 and 3 in pencil, upper left. Title-page and pp. 2 and 3 of text, black ribbon; p. 1 of text, black carbon.

e. "II | Powhatan's Daughter". T.ms., 13p. (black carbon). 13 sheets of typing paper. 21 x 16.2 cm. Sheets numbered 7 through 19 in pencil, upper left, and numbered 10 through 22 in red pencil, lower right. Notations in ink throughout (Crane's hand). Note on p. 19 (numbered in pencil), "Indiana (to come—about 3 pages"). Pinned to pp. 8 and 9 (numbered in pencil) are four glosses to stanzas 1, 6, 7, and 9 of "The Harbor Dawn", typed on light-blue pieces of typing paper of various sizes. There is also additional sheet of typewritten glosses, "THE BRIDGE - Gloss-2-", light-blue typing paper (27 x 21 cm.), containing glosses for "Van Winkle", "The River", and "The Dance".

f. "Indiana". T.ms., 3p. (purple carbon). 3 sheets of typing paper. 27.5 x 21.3 cm. Sheets unnumbered. Signed in ink at end of text.

g. "II | Powhatan's Daughter". T.ms., 13p. (black ribbon). 13 sheets of typing paper. 21 x 16.2 cm. Sheets numbered 1 through 13 in pencil, upper left.

h. "III | Cutty Sark". T.ms., 5p. (black carbon). 5 sheets of typing paper. 21 x 16.2 cm. Sheets numbered 20 through 24 in pencil, upper left. Notations in ink (Crane's hand). "Original version" written in pencil on p. 20, top left (probably Caresse Crosby's hand). Blue pencil line and "Ne pas faire" written in blue pencil along left margin of p. 21.

i. "Cutty Sark". T.ms., 5p. (black ribbon). 5 sheets of typing paper. 21 x 16.2 cm. Sheets numbered 14 through 18 in pencil, upper left.

j. "Cutty Sark". T.ms., 3p. (black ribbon). 3 sheets of typing paper. 27.5 x 21.5 cm. Sheets numbered 1 through 3 in pencil, lower right. Several minor corrections and emendations (Crane's hand in ink). On p. 1, top right, "2nd version rec'd Sept 14. c c" (Caresse Crosby's hand).

k. "IV | Cape Hatteras": Title-page. T.ms., 1p. (black carbon). 1 sheet of typing paper. 21 x 16.2 cm. Sheet numbered 25 in pencil, upper left. Center bottom, canceled in red pencil, "(To come) From five to 8 pages" (Crane's hand in ink).

l. "Cape Hatteras": Title-page. T.ms., 1p. (black ribbon). 1 sheet of typing paper. 21 x 16.2 cm.

m. "IV | Cape Hatteras". T.ms., 7p. (black ribbon and black carbon). 7 sheets of typing paper. 27.8 x 21.3 cm. First sheet, black ribbon, and remainder, black carbon. Title-page and first sheet of text unnumbered; rest of sheets numbered 2 through 6. Corrections and emendations (Crane's hand in ink). On p. [1], top right, "final version" (Crane's hand in ink); "rec'd Sept 30" written in pencil beneath (probably Caresse Crosby's hand). Signed and dated "9/17/29", in ink on p. 6 at end of text.

n. "V | Three Songs". T.ms., 5p. (black ribbon). 5 sheets of typing paper. 21 x 16.2 cm. Sheets numbered 26 through 30 in pencil, upper left. Corrections and emendations (Crane's hand in ink and Caresse Crosby's hand in blue pencil). Text of "Virginia" on pp. 29-30 canceled in blue pencil, and written alongside first stanza on p. 29 in blue pencil "voir nouvelle version" (Caresse Crosby's hand).

o. "Three Songs". T.ms., 5p. (black carbon). 5 sheets of typing paper. 21 x 16.2 cm. Sheets unnumbered.

p. "VI | Quaker Hill"; Title-page. T.ms., 1p. (black ribbon). 1 sheet of white stationery. 18 x 14 cm. Lower center (Crane's hand in ink) "(To come) about 3 pages".

q. "Quaker Hill". T.ms., 3p. (black ribbon). 3 sheets of typing paper. 27.8 x 21.5 cm. Contains title-page and pp. 2–3, stanzas 5–9; p. 1 of text lacking. Two notations and one emendation (Crane's hand in ink). Signed by Crane in ink on p. 3 following text.

r. "VII | The Tunnel". T.ms., 6p. (black ribbon). 6 sheets of typing paper. 21 x 16.2 cm. Sheets numbered 32 through 37 in pencil, upper left. Emendations and notations (Crane's hand in ink).

s. "The Tunnel". T.ms., 6p. (black carbon). 6 sheets of typing paper. 21 x 16.2 cm. Sheets unnumbered.

t. "VIII | Atlantis". T.ms., 5p. (black ribbon). 5 sheets of typing paper. Sheets numbered 38 through 42 in pencil, upper left. Emendations and notations (Crane's hand in ink). Signed and dated on p. 42, "Hart Crane– | Paris – | July 14th '29".

u. "Atlantis". T.ms., 5p. (black carbon). 5 sheets of typing paper. 21 x 16.2 cm. Sheets unnumbered.

B3. *The Bridge.* T.ms., 41p. (black ribbon and black carbon). TxU

Title: *THE BRIDGE:* | A POEM | by | HART CRANE | [epigraph from The Book of Job on three lines] | (title page)

Date: ca. Spring-Fall 1929. (Since text, particularly that of "Cape Hatteras" section, agrees with that published by the Black Sun Press, it would seem likely that type-script could be dated in late 1929; however, numbering of final sections indicates earlier date. Pagination of typescripts not consecutive, suggesting that manuscript comprises work of various dates.)

Contents:

a. Preliminary sheets: Cover title-page containing typed title, "THE | BRIDGE", with device depicting a knot above title and device depicting an anchor beneath, surrounded by single-line border (Crane's hand in pencil); Title-page; Contents page. T.ms., 3p. (black ribbon). 3 sheets of typing paper. 28 x 21.5 cm.

b. "To | Brooklyn Bridge". T.ms., 2p. (black ribbon). 2 sheets of typing paper. 28 x 21.5 cm. Typed upper left on both sheets, "The Bridge - Dedication". Second sheet numbered 2. One emendation (Crane's hand in ink).

c. "I | Ave Maria". T.ms., 3p. (black ribbon). 3 sheets of typing paper. 28 x 21.5 cm. Typed epigraph from Seneca on title-page transcribed beneath in ink (Crane's hand). On verso of third sheet are first 5 lines of stanza 9, typewritten and canceled in pencil. Sheets unnumbered.

d. "II | Powhatan's Daughter". T.ms., 13p. (black ribbon). 13 sheets of typing paper. 28 x 21.5 cm. Various pagings. Emendations (Crane's hand in ink and pencil). Typescript of "The Harbor Dawn" contains first 8 stanzas only, and fifth poem in series, "Indiana", lacking.

e. "III | Cutty Sark". T.ms., 4p. (black carbon). 4 sheets of typing paper. 28 x 21.5 cm. Last two sheets numbered 2 and 3. Notations and emendation (Crane's hand in ink).

f. "IV | Cape Hatteras". T.ms., 5p. (black carbon). 5 sheets of typing paper. 28 x 21.5 cm. Last three sheets numbered 2 through 4. Text lacking for final 6 stanzas. Emendations and corrections (Crane's hand in ink).

g. "Southern Cross". "National Winter Garden". "Virginia". T.ms., 3p. (black ribbon). 3 sheets of typing paper. 28 x 21.5 cm. Each poem typed on separate sheet.

h. "IX | The Tunnel". T.ms., 5p. (black ribbon). 5 sheets of typing paper. 28 x 21.5 cm. Final three sheets numbered 2 through 4. One emendation (Crane's hand in ink).

i. "X | Atlantis". T.ms., 2p. (black ribbon). 2 sheets of typing paper. 28 x 21.5 cm. Text contains first 4 stanzas only. One emendation (Crane's hand in pencil).

B4. *The Bridge.* T.ms., 53p. (black ribbon). NjP

Title: *THE BRIDGE* | A POEM | by HART CRANE | [epigraph from The Book of Job on three lines]

Collation: 53 sheets of typing paper. 27.7 x 21.5 cm. Three holes pierced along left margin. Sheets unnumbered.

Date: ca. Winter 1929–1930. (Note by Allen Tate accompanying manuscript states that Crane gave typescript to him in January, 1930, for purposes of writing his review).

Contents: Typescript of complete poem as published by the Black Sun Press in January 1930. Corrections and emendations (Crane's hand in ink) scattered throughout manuscript. On verso of sheet preceding title-page (Crane's hand in ink), "This MS is property of | Hart Crane | 190 Columbia Heights | Brooklyn N. Y."

Note: Accompanying manuscript are two-page note by Allen Tate recording history of this particular typescript, photograph of the Brooklyn Bridge by Walker Evans attached to sheet bearing bibliographical notations of Black Sun Press and Liveright editions (Crane's hand), and two pages of notes made by Tate as he read poem for first time.

Individual Poems

B5. "To Brooklyn Bridge". T.ms., 2 p. (black ribbon). NNC

Title: DEDICATION | TO | BROOKLYN BRIDGE

First line: How many dawns, chill from his rippling rest

Collation: 2 sheets of tan onionskin paper. 27.8 x 21.5 cm. Second sheet numbered 2. (Enclosed in letter from Crane to Grace Hart Crane, 23 January 1927.)

Date: 23 January 1927.

Contents: Typescript, 11 stanzas of 4 lines each, as published in *The Dial* (June 1927), and varying in several instances from version published in TB, pp. 7–8.

B6. "Ave Maria". A. and t.ms., 2p. (Crane's hand in ink and pencil; black and red ribbon). NNC

First line: And it is ghostly here

Collation: 1 sheet of tan onionskin paper, written on both sides. 27.8 x 21.5 cm.

Date: ca. 1926.

Contents: Worksheet, possibly first draft, containing miscellaneous lines and images and portions of opening and closing lines. (See Fig. 2.)

B7.   "Ave Maria". T.ms., 2p. (black ribbon). NNC

First line: Spun sweat of heaven

Collation: 1 sheet of typing paper, written on both sides. 25.5 x 21.5 cm. Top portion of sheet cut away affecting text on verso.

Date: ca. 1926.

Contents: Worksheets containing primarily drafts of final sections. Alterations and emendations in ink, one in pencil (Crane's hand). On recto, red pencil line drawn alongside stanza beginning "They judge whose strictures of their sight . . . "

B8.   "Ave Maria". T.ms., 1p. (black ribbon). PU

First line: Be with me, Luis de St. Angel, now—

Collation: 1 sheet of typing paper. 28 x 21.5 cm. (At head of letter from Crane to Waldo Frank, 20 March 1926.)

Date: 20 March 1926.

Contents: Early typescript draft of stanzas 1 and 2, 16 lines.

B9.   "Ave Maria". T.ms., 4p. (black ribbon). NNC

Title: I | AVE MARIA

First line: Be with me, Luis de San Angel, now—

Collation: 4 sheets of typing paper. 33 x 21.5 cm. Last three sheets numbered 2 through 4. (With envelope postmarked Patterson, N. Y., 27 January 1927.)

Date: 27 January 1927.

Contents: Typescript as published in *The American Caravan* (1927) and varying from version published in

TB and CP. On top of first sheet, unsigned note to Grace Hart Crane (Crane's hand in ink).

B10. "Ave Maria". T.ms., 4p. (black carbon). TxU

Title: I | AVE MARIA

First line: Be with me, Luis de San Angel, now—

Collation: 4 sheets of typing paper. 28 x 21.5 cm. Last three sheets numbered 2 through 4.

Date: ca. January 1927.

Contents: Typescript as published in *The American Caravan* (1927) and varying from version published in TB and CP.

B11. "The Harbor Dawn". T.ms., 2p. (black ribbon). TxU

Title: II | POWHATAN'S DAUGHTER | (1)

First line: In sleep,—as though a shadow bloomed aloud,

Collation: 2 sheets of typing paper. 28 x 21.5 cm. Second sheet numbered 2.

Date: ca. Spring 1927.

Contents: Early typescript, 24 lines in 7 stanzas of varying lengths.

B12. "The Harbor Dawn". T. and a.ms., 2p. (black ribbon; Crane's hand in ink). NNC

Title: THE HARBOR DAWN

First line: Through sleep, and pensively—a tide of voices—

Collation: 1 sheet of typing paper, written on both sides. 27.8 x 21.5 cm.

Date: ca. 1927.

Contents: On recto, late typewritten draft of first 6 stanzas, with emendations in ink and pencil (Crane's hand); complete text canceled in pencil. Typed on top of sheet, "The Bridge - II Powhatan's Daughter -1". On verso, outlines for "Cape Hatteras" and "The Bridge" (Crane's hand in ink).

B13. "The River". T. and a.ms., 2p. (black ribbon; Crane's hand in ink and pencil). NNC

First line: They lurk across her—knowing her yonder breast

Collation: 1 sheet of typing paper, written on both sides. 27.8 x 21.4 cm.

Date: ca. July 1926–July 1927.

Contents: On recto, typewritten drafts of portions of stanzas 8 and 5; in pencil lower left, "M L Emmons" (probably Crane's hand). On verso, two drafts of last 4 lines of stanza 12, one typewritten and another in ink (Crane's hand); also two fragments related to "The River" (Crane's hand in ink and pencil).

B14. "The River". T.ms., 1p. (black ribbon). NNC

First line: And in the circuit of the lamp's thin flame

Collation: 1 sheet of typing paper. 27.8 x 21.5 cm.

Date: ca. July 1926–July 1927.

Contents: Typewritten draft of stanzas 9 through 13; emendations and notations (Crane's hand in pencil). "3" typed top center.

B15. "The River". A. and t.ms., 2p. (Crane's hand in ink and pencil; black ribbon). NNC

First line: damp tonnage and alluvial march of days

Collation: 1 sheet of typing paper. 32.8 x 21.5 cm.

Date: ca. July 1926–July 1927.

Contents: On recto, drafts of five final stanzas (Crane's hand in ink and pencil); on top of sheet several notes and lines from "Van Winkle". On verso, typewritten and handwritten drafts of stanzas 10 and 11; on bottom three rows of figures (Crane's hand in ink). Inscribed on recto, top right, "To Samuel Loveman | from | Hart Crane | December 31, 1929". (See Fig. 3.)

B16. "The River". T.ms., 1p. (black ribbon). NNC

Title: THE RIVER

First line: You will not hear it as the sea, though stone

Collation: 1 sheet of typing paper. 27.8 x 21.4 cm. (Enclosed in letter from Crane to Grace Hart Crane, 18 June 1927.)

Date: 18 June 1927.

Contents: Typescript of stanzas 14 through 20 as published in *The Second American Caravan* (1928). Note lower left (Crane's hand in ink). Typed on top of sheet above title, "FROM THE BRIDGE: Section II, Powhatan's Daughter, 3".

B17. "The River". T.ms., 4p. (black ribbon). NNC

Title: THE RIVER

First line: Stick your patent name on a signboard

Collation: 4 sheets of typing paper. 27.8 x 21.5 cm. Last three sheets numbered 2 through 4. (Enclosed in letter from Crane to Mrs. T. W. Simpson, 4 July 1927.)

Date: 4 July 1927.

Contents: Late typewritten draft which occasionally varies from published version. Typed on top of first sheet, "The Bridge II - Powhatan's Daughter - 3". Typed to left of stanza 9, "(new stanza)"; one correction in ink (Crane's hand), stanza 9, line 9. On bottom of p.4 (Crane's hand in ink), "by Hart Crane | Patterson, NY".

B18. "The River". T.ms., 6p. (black ribbon). NNC

Title: III | THE RIVER

First line: Stick your patent name on a signboard

Collation: 4 sheets of typing paper, the first and last written on both sides. 27.8 x 21.5 cm. Last two sheets are numbered 3 and 4.

Date: ca. July 1927.

Contents: Late typescript draft which occasionally varies from published version. On verso of first sheet are two typescript drafts of stanza 10 with several lines in ink and pencil (Crane's hand). On verso of p. 4 are two drafts of stanza 9, one typewritten and other in ink (Crane's hand). Emendations and notations throughout (Crane's hand in ink and pencil).

B18a. "The River". T.ms., 4p. (black ribbon). NNC

Title: THE RIVER

First line: Stick your patent name on a signboard

Collation: 4 sheets of typing paper. 27.8 x 21.5 cm. Last three sheets numbered 2 through 4. (Enclosed in letter from Crane to Isidor Schneider, 6 November 1927.)

Date: 6 November 1927.

Contents: Late typescript which agrees with the published versions. One emendation in ink on p. 4 (Crane's hand). Typed on bottom of p. 4 following text, "Hart Crane, | RFD – Patterson, NY".

B19. "The Dance". T.ms., 1p. (black ribbon). PU

Title: II POWHATAN'S DAUGHTER -pt 4 -pg 3

First line: A birth kneels. All her whistling fingers fly.

Collation: 1 sheet of typing paper. 28 x 21.5 cm.

Date: ca. June 1927.

Contents: Typescript of stanzas 13 through 19; one correction (Crane's hand in pencil). Upper left (Crane's hand in pencil), "Substitute for former pg 3". Typed on bottom of sheet is note concerning Maquokeeta, mentioned in stanza 15.

B20. "The Dance". T.ms., 4p. (black ribbon and carbon). TxU

First line: The swift red flesh, a winter king,—

Collation: 4 sheets of typing paper. 28 x 21.5 cm. Sheets numbered 1 through 4. Page 3 carbon copy and the other three sheets black ribbon.

Date: ca. July 1927.

Contents: Late typescript. On top of each page is typed "II Powhatan's Daughter -pt 4", and at head of text on p. 1 is typed "(4)". On p. 1, upper left, is note to Allen Tate; and on p. 3 (Crane's hand in pencil), "Substitute for former pg. 3".

B21. "Indiana". T.ms., 3p. (black ribbon). ICU

Title: ELDORADO

First line: The morning glory, climbing the morning long

Collation: 3 sheets of typing paper. 25.5 x 20 cm. Last two sheets numbered 2 and 3.

Date: ca. Fall 1929.

Contents: Typescript of "Eldorado" (later titled "Indiana") as published in *Poetry* (April 1930). Typed on first sheet, upper right, "by Hart Crane, | 190 Columbia Heights, | Brooklyn, N.Y." Signed in ink on p. 3 following text.

B22. "Indiana". T.ms., 2p. (black ribbon). ICU

Title: E L D O R A D O

First line: The morning glory, climbing the morning long

Collation: 2 sheets of typing paper. 25.5 x 20 cm. Second sheet numbered 2.

Date: ca. Fall 1929.

Contents: Typescript as published in *Poetry* (April 1930). Editorial markings and notations throughout.

B23. "Cutty Sark". T.ms., 3p. (black ribbon). ICU

Title: C U T T Y S A R K

First line: I met a man in South Street, tall—

Collation: 3 sheets of typing paper. 25.7 x 20.5 cm. Last two sheets numbered 2 and 3.

Date: April 1927.

Contents: Typescript as published in *Poetry* (October 1927). On p. 1 upper left, "final version" (Crane's hand in ink). Upper left "Acd. Mar. 23, '27" and upper right "Revision received Apr. 6, '27" (unknown hand in ink). Editorial markings and notations throughout.

B24. "Cape Hatteras". A. and t.ms., 15p. (Crane's hand in ink and pencil; black ribbon). NNC

Title: *CAPE HATTERAS* [Crane's hand in ink on cover of folder]

Collation: 15 sheets of typing paper, white and blue, of which 3 written on both sides. Sizes of sheets range from 27 x 21 cm. to 27.8 x 21.5 cm. Sheets unnumbered and enclosed in manilla folder with title (as above) and several lines in ink and pencil (Crane's hand), latter canceled heavily in red pencil.

Date: ca. 1927–August 1929.

Contents: Worksheets of drafts and fragments. Typescript sections bear numerous alterations and emendations in ink and pencil, as well as notations in blue pencil and underscorings in red pencil.

B25. "Cape Hatteras". A.ms., 2p. (Crane's hand in ink). NNC

Title: Freedom, A Chemical Dispensation

First line: The smoke dries on the ceiling of our words

Collation: 1 sheet of typing paper, written on both sides. 27.7 x 21.3 cm.

Date: ca. 1927.

Contents: Early draft of first section. On recto, 14 lines with three alterations in ink (Crane's hand). On verso, 2 lines in ink and 7 words in pencil (Crane's hand).

B26. "Cape Hatteras". T. and a.ms., 1p. (black ribbon; Crane's hand in ink and pencil). NNC

First line: Not wings alone, but rhythm of wings

Collation: 1 sheet of typing paper. 27.8 x 21.5 cm.

Date: ca. 1927–August 1929.

Contents: Worksheet of drafts for section dealing with airplane, 13 typewritten lines, and 13 lines (Crane's hand in ink and pencil); double red pencil lines drawn along left margin and "doubtful" written beneath in blue pencil (probably Crane's hand). On verso, two pencil sketches.

B27. "Cape Hatteras". A.ms., 1p. (Crane's hand in pencil). NNC

First line: There in the fleeing balconies of your wings

Collation: 1 sheet of light-blue typing paper. 26.8 x 21 cm.

Date: ca. 1927–August 1929.

Contents: Draft of fragment of section dealing with airplane, 5 lines (Crane's hand in pencil). On bottom of sheet, "Hopital de St. Mandrier" (Crane's hand in ink).

B28. "Cape Hatteras". A.ms., 1p. (Crane's hand in pencil). NNC

First line: Augeries are stripped of space

Collation: 1 sheet of tan paper. 21.5 x 14 cm.

Date: ca. 1927–August 1929.

Contents: Fragment of 5 lines related to section dealing with airplane.

B29. "Cape Hatteras". T.ms., 1p. (black ribbon). NNC

Title: NOTES | *Cape Hatteras section - (the forge)*

First lines: Whitman approaches the bed of a dying *(southern)* soldier - scene is | in a Washington hospital.

Collation: 1 sheet of tan onionskin paper. 27.8 x 21.5 cm.

Date: ca. 1927.

Contents: Three paragraphs of notes for section dealing with Walt Whitman, as published in BW, p. 260.

B30. "Cape Hatteras". A. and t.ms., 1p. (Crane's hand in ink and pencil; black ribbon). NNC

First line: Thou, as the junction, there, of speed

Collation: 1 sheet of typing paper. 27.8 x 21.5 cm.

Date: ca. 1927–August 1929.

Contents: Worksheet of drafts for stanza 11 dealing with Walt Whitman. Multiple red pencil lines drawn alongisde each stanza, several lines underscored in red pencil.

B31. "Cape Hatteras". T. and a.ms., 2p. (black ribbon; Crane's hand in pencil). NNC

First line: O thou art lovable — as fire and sprite,

Collation: 1 sheet of typing paper, written on both sides. 27 x 21 cm.

Date: ca. 1927–August 1929.

Contents: On recto, draft of stanza 11, section dealing with Walt Whitman, 12 lines in 2 stanzas; on bottom of sheet, 2 lines in red pencil heavily canceled in red pencil (Crane's hand). On verso, worksheet of drafts of sections from "Ave Maria" and "Harbor Dawn" (Crane's hand in pencil).

B32. "Cape Hatteras". T. and a.ms., 1p. (black ribbon; Crane's hand in ink). NNC

First line: Thou and adorations, of the golden breakless chain

Collation: 1 sheet of typing paper. 27.5 x 21.4 cm.

Date: ca. 1927–August 1929.

Contents: Draft of fragment of final section of poem, 7 typewritten lines and 5 lines (Crane's hand in ink).

B33. "Cape Hatteras". A.ms., 1p. (Crane's hand in ink). NNC

First line: That euphony the firmament defrauds us of
Collation: 1 sheet of typing paper, written on both sides.
27.5 x 21.3 cm.

Date: ca. August 1929.

Contents: On recto, draft of fragment of section dealing
with airplane, 7 lines (Crane's hand in ink). On verso,
typewritten list of nine names with heading "Copies of
the Bridge to be sent at once".

B34. "Cape Hatteras". T.ms., 1p. (black ribbon). NNC

Title: CAPE HATTERAS

First lines: Imponderable the dinosaur who | sinks slow,

Collation: 1 segmented sheet comprising 2 sheets of
white and 4 sheets of tan typing paper. Overall dimen-
sions, 137.5 x 21.5 cm.

Date: ca. Summer 1929.

Contents: Late typescript draft, text differing somewhat
from final version sent to Caresse Crosby and published
by the Black Sun Press, and version published in the
Saturday Review of Literature (March 15, 1930). Corrections and emendations (Crane's hand in ink and
pencil). On bottom of verso (Crane's hand in pencil),
"Agnes O'Neil | Point Pleasant | N. J."

B35. "Cape Hatteras". T.ms., 6p. (black ribbon). ICarbS

Title: *CAPE | HATTERAS*

First line: Imponderable the dinosaur

Collation: 6 sheets of typing paper. 27.5 x 21.5 cm. Last
five sheets numbered 2 through 6.

Date: ca. August 1929.

Contents: Late typescript draft of complete poem; several corrections and emendations (Crane's hand in ink). On p. 1 upper right (Caresse Crosby's hand in pencil), "version rec'd Sept 5 *not* final". Signed "Hart Crane" on p. 6 following text.

B36. "Cape Hatteras". T.ms., 2p. (black ribbon). ICarbS

First line: Thou, there beyond—

Collation: 1 sheet of typing paper, 27.5 x 21.5 cm., and 1 half-sheet of typing paper, 16 x 21.5 cm. Sheets numbered 1 and 2.

Date: ca. September 1929.

Contents: Late typescript draft of final 68 lines; corrections and emendations throughout (Crane's hand in ink). On p. 1 upper right, "received Sept 14", and along left margin, "1st version, the 2nd corrected version is with the poems" (Caresse Crosby's hand in ink and pencil). Probably version referred to in letter from Crane to Caresse Crosby, 6 September 1929 (see LHC, pp. 345–46).

B37. "Three Songs". T.ms., 3p. (black ribbon). NNC

Title: THE BRIDGE - V - THREE SONGS

First line: I wanted you, nameless Woman of the South

Collation: 3 sheets of typing paper. 27.8 x 21.5 cm.

Date: 1927. (Dated in pencil in upper right of first sheet, unknown hand. Note from Crane on the first sheet refers to poems' publication in July 1927 issue of *The Calendar*.

Contents: Typescript of "Three Songs", including "Southern Cross", "National Winter Garden", and "Virginia", each on separate sheet, texts differing slightly from published ones. On top of first sheet is signed note in ink from Crane to Grace Hart Crane beginning "These things from The Bridge have just appeared in The Calendar (a London quarterly)..."

B38. "National Winter Garden". T.ms., 1p. (black ribbon). NNC

Title: *National | Winter | Garden*

First line: Outspoken buttocks in pink heads

Collation: 1 sheet of tan onionskin paper. 27.8 x 21.5 cm.

Date: ca. 1926.

Contents: Typescript differing in several instances from the published version, 7 stanzas of 4 lines each. Typed lower right, "Hart Crane", top center, "2", and top right, "Three Songs from 'The Bridge' -pg 2".

B39. "Virginia". T.ms., 1p. (purple carbon). NNC

Title: *VIRGINIA*

First lines: O rain at seven, | Pay-check at eleven—

Collation: 1 sheet of typing paper. 27.5 x 21.3 cm.

Date: ca. September 1929.

Contents: Carbon copy typescript; emendations and notations (Crane's hand in ink). On bottom of sheet typed note signed in ink concerning setting of poem in type, probably addressed to Caresse Crosby. Beneath typed note is another note (Crane's hand in ink), "Please use this copy for text and punctuation also". Probably new version referred to in manuscript for "The Bridge" sent to the Crosbys (see item B2n); text agrees with that published in Black Sun Press edition and varies in several instances from that published in *The Calendar* (1927).

B40. "Quaker Hill". T.ms., 1p. (black ribbon). NNC

First line: Here space is offered in a idiom (a clause) [Crane's hand in ink]

Collation: 1 sheet of typing paper. 27.5 x 21.5 cm.

Date: ca. Autumn 1929.

Contents: Typescript draft of first 2 stanzas, 16 type-written lines and 6 lines (Crane's hand in ink). Emendations in ink and notations in red pencil. Text on lower half of sheet canceled in ink and blue pencil. (See Fig. 4.)

B41. "Quaker Hill". A.ms., 1p. (Crane's hand in pencil). NNC

First line: Cider, that sumptuous lean line

Collation: 1 sheet of typing paper. 27.5 x 21.5 cm.

Date: ca. Autumn 1929.

Contents: Draft of fragment of stanza 2, 5 lines. At center top, "unhusked" (Crane's hand in ink).

B42. "Quaker Hill". A.ms., 1p. (Crane's hand in ink). NNC

First line: Some of us have this sense but — to know

Collation: 1 sheet of tan notebook paper. 21 x 14.5 cm.

Date: ca. Autumn 1929.

Contents: Worksheet for stanza 7, 14 lines.

B43. "Quaker Hill". T.ms., 1p. (black ribbon). NNC

First line: Shoulder the curse of sundered parentage

Collation: 1 sheet of typing paper. 27.5 x 21.3 cm.

Date: ca. Autumn 1929.

Contents: Typescript drafts of last 4 lines of stanza 7, first 4 lines of stanza 4 (2 drafts), and last 4 lines of stanza 4; emendations (Crane's hand in ink).

B44. "Quaker Hill". T.ms., 1p. (black ribbon). NNC

Title: Quaker Hill—midway notes [Crane's hand in ink]

First line: The resigned factions of the dead preside

Collation: 1 sheet of typing paper. 27.5 x 21.3 cm.

Date: ca. Autumn 1929.

Contents: Typescript drafts of stanzas 6 and 7, 24 lines; with additional line, "The Promised Land, the mandate, the legacy" (Crane's hand in ink), in center of sheet and underscored in red. Emendations (Crane's hand in ink and pencil).

B45. "Quaker Hill". T.ms., 1p. (black ribbon). NNC

Title: QUAKER HILL — NOTES 2

First line: Then as the eyes that turn round the sulphurous blaze

Collation: 1 sheet of typing paper. 27.5 x 21.5 cm.

Date: ca. Autumn 1929.

Contents: Typescript notes for final 2 stanzas, 16 lines.

B46. "Quaker Hill". T. and a.ms., 1p. (black ribbon; Crane's hand in ink). NNC

First line: O from the hawk's far soaring view

Collation: 1 sheet of typing paper. 27.5 x 21.3 cm.

Date: ca. Autumn 1929.

Contents: Typescript draft of stanza 8, 11 lines, of which first 3 lines canceled in ink; emendations (Crane's hand in ink). Following draft of stanza 8 is draft of stanza 9, 9 lines (Crane's hand in ink).

B47. "Quaker Hill". T.ms., 4p. (black ribbon). ICarbS

Title: QUAKER HILL

First line: Perspective never withers from their eyes;

Collation: 4 sheets of typing paper. 27.5 x 21.5 cm. Last two sheets numbered 2 and 3.

Date: ca. Autumn 1929.

Contents: Typescript of complete poem with stanza 5 of published version lacking. Typescript includes unnumbered title-page.

B48. "Quaker Hill". T.ms., 1p. (black ribbon). NNC

Title: QUAKER HILL

Collation: 1 sheet of typing paper. 27.5 x 21.3 cm.

Date: ca. Autumn 1929.

Contents: Typescript title-page containing epigraphs from Isadora Duncan and Emily Dickinson. One emendation (Crane's hand in pencil).

B49. "The Tunnel". T.ms., 4p. (black ribbon). TxU

Title: THE TUNNEL

First line: Performances, assortments, résumés—

Collation: 4 sheets of typing paper. 28 x 21.5 cm. Last three sheets numbered 2 through 4.

Date: ca. Autumn-Winter 1926.

Contents: Early typescript, varying from version published in *The Criterion* (November 1927).

B50. "Atlantis". A.ms., 1p. (Crane's hand in ink). CtY

First line: And midway on that structure I would stand

Collation: 1 sheet of typing paper. 22.3 x 17.5 cm. (Incorporated into letter from Crane to Wilbur Underwood, 20 February 1923.)

Date: February 20, 1923.

Contents: Early handwritten draft of 13 lines from final portions of poem as published in BW, p. 425.

B51. "Atlantis". T.ms., 1p. (black ribbon). CtY

First line: The baited rock precipitate with sound

Collation: 1 sheet of ruled paper. 31.5 x 20 cm. (Enclosed in letter from Crane to Alfred Stieglitz, 4 July 1923.)

Date: 4 July 1923.

Contents: Early typescript draft as published in BW, pp. 426–28.

B52. "Atlantis". T.ms., 1p. (black ribbon). TNF

Title: from THE BRIDGE

First line: The hand you carry to the rock knows lime

Collation: 2 sheets of typing paper. 27.5 x 21.3 cm. Sheets unnumbered.

Date: ca. Summer 1923.

Contents: Early typescript drafts, 56 lines in 6 stanzas of varying lengths. First 43 lines correspond to those published in BW, pp. 428–29. Manuscript is inscribed in ink by Crane to Jean Toomer on second sheet following text, "A copy for Jean, | with (I hope) improvements | later — | but always, Hart".

B53. "Atlantis". T.ms., 2p. (black ribbon). NNC

First line: The grinding whirr of cassions, torrid sledge,

Collation: 1 sheet of typing paper, written on both sides. 27.7 x 21.3 cm.

Date: ca. 1926.

Contents: On recto, drafts of 3 stanzas, 23 lines, with "3" typed on top of sheet; emendations (Crane's hand in ink). On verso, a draft of stanza 4, 8 lines, and 3 lines (Crane's hand in ink), unrelated to stanza 4. Drafts published in BW, pp. 429–30, 434.

B54. "Atlantis". T.ms., 4p. (black ribbon). PU

Title: Bridge - finale

First line: Through the twined cable strands, the arching path

Collation: 4 sheets of typing paper. 28 x 21.5 cm. Last three sheets numbered 2 through 4. (Enclosed in letter from Crane to Waldo Frank, 18 January 1926.)

Date: 18 January 1926.

Contents: Typescript draft of 10 stanzas varying in length from 8 to 10 lines, as published in BW, pp. 430–32. Two corrections (Crane's hand in ink).

B55. "Atlantis". T.ms., 2p. (black ribbon). NNC

First line: Through the twined cable strands, the arching path

Collation: 1 sheet of typing paper, written on both sides. 27.5 x 21.3 cm.

Date: ca. Spring–Summer 1926.

Contents: Typescript drafts of first 4 stanzas, 3 stanzas on recto, 1 stanza on verso, as published in BW, pp.

432–37. Emendations and additions (Crane's hand in ink).

B56. "Atlantis". T.ms., 2p. (black ribbon). NNC

First line: Sheerly the eyes are poured in avenues

Collation: 1 sheet of light-green typing paper, written on both sides. 27.8 x 21.3 cm.

Date: ca. Spring–Summer 1926.

Contents: On recto, typescript drafts of stanza 4 and 2 additional stanzas relating to second half of poem; emendations (Crane's hand in ink). On verso, 2 typescript drafts of stanza 4; emendations, additions, and 4 lines (Crane's hand in ink). Drafts published in BW, pp. 433–34.

B57. "Atlantis". T.ms., 1p. (black ribbon). NNC

First line: Sheerly the eyes are spilled in avenues,

Collation: 1 sheet of typing paper. 27.7 x 21.3 cm.

Date: ca. Spring–Summer 1926.

Contents: Typescript drafts of stanza 4, 16 lines, as published in BW, p. 435; typescript revisions.

B58. "Atlantis". T.ms., 2p. (black ribbon). NNC

First line: Sheerly the eyes are spilled in avenues,

Collation: 1 sheet of typing paper, written on both sides. 27.7 x 21.3 cm.

Date: ca. Spring–Summer 1926.

Contents: On recto, three typescript drafts of stanza 4, 22 lines. On verso, one typescript draft of stanza 4, 12 lines. Typescript revisions throughout. Drafts published in BW, pp. 435–37.

B59. "Atlantis". T.ms., 4p. (black ribbon). PU

Title: *BRIDGE - Final Section*

First line: Through the twined cable strands, the arching path

Collation: 4 sheets of typing paper. 28 x 21.5 cm. Last three sheets numbered 2 through 4. (Enclosed in letter from Crane to Waldo Frank, 3 August 1926.)

Date: 3 August 1926.

Contents: Late typescript draft, 11 stanzas of 8 lines each, as published in BW, pp. 437-40.

C.

"KEY WEST"

Complete Manuscripts

C1. *Key West*. T. and a.ms., 32p. (black ribbon and black carbon; Crane's hand in ink and pencil). NNC

Title: *KEY WEST* | *An Island Sheaf* | by | Hart Crane | [asterisk] | [epigraph from Blake on four lines]

Collation: 32 sheets of typing paper. Various sizes. Sheets unnumbered and enclosed in manilla folder with title, epigraph from Blake, and notes by Crane and Peggy Baird in ink; pasted on inside front cover of folder is sheet of red paper with woodcut of the Madonna printed in black.

Date: ca. 1927–April 1932.

Contents: Typescripts and handwritten drafts of all poems in "Key West" section of CP, with exceptions of "The Broken Tower", "The Phantom Bark", and "March".

a. Title-page. T.ms., 1p. (black ribbon). 1 sheet of typing paper. 27.8 x 21.5 cm.

b. Contents page. T.ms., 1p. (black ribbon). 1 sheet of typing paper. 27.8 x 21.5 cm.

c. "O Carib Isle!" T.ms., 1p. (black carbon). 1 sheet of legal size typing paper. 33 x 21.3 cm. Typed lower right, "Grand Cayman | July '26 | Transition (Paris) | April '27". On verso, title written in ink and underlined (Crane's hand).

d. "O Carib Isle!" T.ms., 1p. (black ribbon). 1 sheet of typing paper. 27.5 x 21.5 cm. Lower right, "terrapins" (Crane's hand in ink).

e. "O Carib Isle!" T.ms., 1p. (black ribbon). 1 sheet of typing paper. 27.8 x 21.4 cm. One emendation (Crane's hand in ink). Typed lower right, "Hart Crane".

f. "The Mermen". T.ms., 1p. (black ribbon). 1 sheet of typing paper. 27.8 x 21.4 cm. One addition (Crane's hand in pencil).

g. "To the Cloud Juggler". T.ms., 1p. (black carbon). 1 sheet of typing paper. 27.8 x 21.5 cm. Blue checkmark, upper left. Lower left, "Sent to Caresse | January 23rd" (Crane's hand in ink).

h. "The Mango Tree". T.ms., 1p. (black ribbon). 1 sheet of typing paper. 27.8 x 21.5 cm. Upper right, checkmark in pencil. Typed lower right, "Hart Crane".

i. "The Mango Tree". T.ms., 1p. (black ribbon). 1 sheet of typing paper. 27.8 x 21.7 cm. Typed lower right, "Hart Crane".

j. "The Mango Tree". T.ms., 1p. (black carbon). 1 sheet of onionskin paper. 28 x 21.5 cm. Carbon copy of previous item.

k. "Quarry". T.ms., 1p. (black ribbon). 1 sheet of typing paper. 27.8 x 21.5 cm. One correction (Crane's hand in ink). Identical with poem later titled "Island Quarry".

l. "Old Song". T.ms., 1p. (black ribbon). 1 sheet of typing paper. 27.8 x 21.5 cm. Typed in red lower right, "New Republic | Aug. '27".

m. "The Idiot". T.ms., 1p. (black ribbon). 1 sheet of typing paper. 27.8 x 21.5 cm. One correction in ink and one in pencil (Crane's hand).

n. "The Idiot". T.ms., 1p. (black ribbon). 1 sheet of typing paper. 27.8 x 21.5 cm. Drafts of two lines and several emendations (Crane's hand in ink).

o. "A Name For All". T.ms., 1p. (black carbon). 1 sheet of typing paper. 27.8 x 21.5 cm. Typed upper left "Hart Crane | c/o Guaranty Trust Co. | Pall Mall, London".

p. "Overheard". T.ms., 1p. (black carbon). 1 sheet of typing paper. 27.8 x 21.5 cm. Typed lower right, "Hart Crane", and lower left (Crane's hand in ink), "Uncle Zeff in Cuba". Identical with poem later titled "Bacardi Spread the Eagle's Wings".

q. "Imperator Victus". T.ms., 1p. (black ribbon). 1 sheet of typing paper. 27.8 x 21.5 cm. Emendations (Crane's hand in pencil).

r. "Royal Palm". T.ms., 1p. (black ribbon). 1 sheet of typing paper. 27.8 x 21.5 cm. One correction in ink (Crane's hand).

s. "The Air Plant". T.ms., 1p. (black ribbon). 1 sheet of typing paper. 27 x 21 cm. Lower right, "Dial" underlined in pencil (probably Crane's hand).

t. "The Air Plant". T.ms., 1p. (black ribbon). 1 sheet of typing paper. 27.8 x 21.5 cm. One correction in pencil (probably Crane's hand).

u. "The Air Plant". T.ms., 1p. (black carbon). 1 sheet of typing paper. 27.8 x 21.5 cm. Typed lower right, "Hart Crane, | RFD - Patterson, N.Y. | as sent to Criterion | July 16th".

v. "The Hour". T.ms., 1p. (black ribbon). 1 sheet of typing paper. 27.8 x 21.5 cm. Entire text canceled in pencil. Early version of "The Hurricane".

w. "The Hurricane". T.ms., 1p. (black ribbon). 1 sheet of typing paper. 27.8 x 21.5 cm. Title underlined in red pencil. Upper right, "final version" underlined twice in red pencil (Crane's hand in ink). Typed upper left, "Hart Crane, | 110 Columbia Heights, | Brooklyn, N.Y." Lower right, "See New Republic version en sequitur" (Crane's hand in pencil). Two corrections in text (Crane's hand in ink).

x. "Key West". A.ms., 2p. (Crane's hand in ink). 1 sheet of typing paper, written on both sides. 27.5 x 21.3 cm. Early worksheet containing notes and 19 lines. (See Fig 5.)

y. "Key West". A. and t.ms., 1 p. (Crane's hand in ink; black ribbon). 1 sheet of typing paper. 27.5 x 21.3 cm. Draft, 16 typewritten lines and 5 lines (Crane's hand in ink). Emendations (Crane's hand in ink). (See Fig. 6.)

z. "Key West". T.ms., 1p. (black ribbon). 1 sheet of typing paper. 28 x 21.5 cm. Alterations in ink (Crane's hand), and signed lower right, "Hart Crane" (unknown hand in pencil).

aa. "And Bees Of Paradise". A. and t.ms., 2p. (Crane's hand in ink; black ribbon). 1 sheet of typing paper, written on both sides. 27.8 x 21.5 cm. On recto, typescript with title and two emendations (Crane's hand in pencil), two pencil sketches lower left, and date, "7/28/27", typed lower right; former title, "By the Dove Filled", typed at head of poem, canceled in pencil, and new title written above. On verso, draft of 8 lines (Crane's hand in ink).

bb. "To Emily Dickinson". T.ms., 1p. (black ribbon). 1 sheet of typing paper. 27.8 x 21.5 cm. One emendation in pencil (Crane's hand). Typed lower right, "The Nation | June 29th, '27", red ribbon.

cc. "Moment Fugue". T.ms., 1p. (black ribbon). 1 sheet of typing paper. 27.8 x 21.5 cm. Typed upper left, "Hart Crane, | Patterson, N.Y."

dd. "By Nilus Once I Knew . . . " T.ms., 1p. (black ribbon). 1 sheet of typing paper. 27.5 x 21.3 cm. Two emendations (Crane's hand in pencil), and signed in pencil, "Hart Crane" (unknown hand).

ee. "To Shakespeare". T.ms., 1p. (black ribbon). 1 sheet of typing paper. 27.8 x 21.5 cm. Emendations in ink (Crane's hand). Typed lower right, "Hart

Crane, | RFD | Patterson, NY". On verso, brief note in pencil (Crane's hand).

ff. "The Tree: Great William". T.ms., 1p. (black ribbon). 1 sheet of typing paper. 27.5 x 21.3 cm. Title underlined and several emendations (Crane's hand in ink and pencil). Upper left, "H. Crane" underlined. One line (Crane's hand in ink) at bottom of sheet. Variation of "To Shakespeare", as published in CP, pp. 133–34. On verso, brief note (Crane's hand in pencil).

C2. *Key West*. T.ms., 34p. (black ribbon). NNC

Title: *KEY WEST* | *AN ISLAND SHEAF* | by | Hart Crane | [asterisk] | [epigraph from Blake on four lines]

Collation: 17 sheets of ruled notebook paper with 2 punched holes along left margin. 26.5 x 20.3 cm. In "Banner Note Book No. 12960" (ring binder), boards covered in black cloth, and with two metal rings; white label on front cover on which is written in block letters "Hart Crane's Poems | Original Mns. | G. H. C." (Grace Hart Crane's hand in ink). Sheets numbered in pencil on both rectos and versos (probably Grace Hart Crane's hand).

Date: ca. May–July 1932. (During months following Crane's death, Grace Hart Crane transcribed uncollected poems and sent them to Waldo Frank for collected edition. Manuscript containing 13 poems received by Frank on July 8 at Truro, Mass., as he states in letter to Mrs. Crane, 9 July 1932, in collection at NNC. This manuscript can be dated in this period.)

Contents: 1. Title-page; 2. blank; 3. "The Idiot". (Three corrections in pencil); 4. blank; 5. "The Mermen". (One correction in pencil); 6. blank; 7. "Old Song"; 8. blank; 9. "The Mango Tree"; 10. blank; 11. "A Name For

All"; 12. blank; 13. "Bacardi Spreads the Eagle's Wings"; 14. blank; 15. "To Emily Dickinson"; 16. blank; 17. "Moment Fugue". (Two notations in pencil); 18. blank; 19. "The Air Plant"; 20–21. blank; 22. "Island Quarry"; 23. "Royal Palm"; 24. blank; 25. "The Hurricane"; 26–30. blank; 31. "O Carib Isle!"; 32–33. blank; 34. Several lines in red pencil (unknown hand).

Individual Poems

C3. "Key West". T.ms., 1p. (black ribbon). NNC

Title: *KEY WEST*

First line: Here has my salient faith annealed me.

Collation: 1 sheet of typing paper. 26.8 x 20.5 cm.

Contents: Typescript, 4 stanzas of 4 lines each. Typed lower right, "Hart Crane | (Copy)".

Note: Copy made by Samuel Loveman in 1932. NNC also has carbon copy of typescript. Poem written by Crane ca. 1927.

C4. "O Carib Isle!" T.ms., 1p. (black ribbon). NNC

Title: O CARIB ISLE!

First line: The tarantula rattling at the lily's foot,

Collation: 1 sheet of typing paper. 27.8 x 21.5 cm. (Enclosed in letter from Crane to Grace Hart Crane, 19 March 1927.)

Date: 19 March 1927.

Contents: Typescript, 31 lines in 7 stanzas, as published in *transition* (April 1927) but varying from version published in CP, pp. 114–15.

C5. "O Carib Isle!" A.ms., 2p. (Crane's hand in ink). ICarbS

Title: *O Carib Isle!*

First line: The tarantula rattling at the lily's foot,

Collation: 2 sheets of typing paper. 27 x 21 cm. Second sheet numbered 2.

Date: ca. Autumn 1926.

Contents: Early handwritten draft, 31 lines in 7 stanzas, same text as item C6. On p. 2, lower right, "Hart Crane | *Grand Cayman* | W.I. | for Harry and Caresse Crosby" (Crane's hand in ink).

C6. "O Carib Isle!" T.ms., 1p. (black carbon). TxU

Title: *O CARIB ISLE!*

First line: The tarantula rattling at the lily's foot,

Collation: 1 sheet of typing paper. 28 x 21.5 cm.

Date: ca. Autumn 1926.

Contents: Early typescript draft, 31 lines in 7 stanzas, same text as item C5. One emendation in ink (Crane's hand). Typed lower right, "*Grand Cayman, West Indies* | by Hart Crane."

C7. "O Carib Isle!" T.ms., 1p. (black ribbon). ICU

Title: *O CARIB ISLE!*

First line: The tarantula rattling at the lily's foot,

Collation: 1 sheet of typing paper. 23 x 19.5 cm.

Date: ca. March 1927.

Contents: Typescript, 31 lines in 7 stanzas, as published in *Poetry* (October 1927) but varying from version published in CP, pp. 114–15. Typed lower right, "by Hart Crane". Editorial markings and notations throughout.

C8.   "O Carib Isle!" A.ms., 1p. (Crane's hand in ink). NSyU

Title: *O Carib Isle!*

First line: The tarantula rattling at the lily's foot,

Collation: 1 sheet of typing paper. 27.8 x 21.5 cm. (Enclosed in letter from Crane to John S. Mayfield, 6 November 1927.)

Date: 6 November 1927.

Contents: Holograph manuscript of stanzas 1, 2, 3, 6, and 7, varying from version published in *transition* (April 1927). Signed lower right, "Hart Crane" and lower left, *"For John S. Mayfield"* (Crane's hand in ink).

C9.   "O Carib Isle!" T.ms., 1p. (black ribbon). ICU

Title: O C A R I B I S L E !

First line: The tarantula rattling at the lily's foot

Collation: 1 sheet of typing paper. 23 x 19.5 cm.

Date: ca. 1927.

Contents: Typescript, 35 lines in 7 stanzas of varying lengths, varying from version published in CP, pp. 114–15; one emendation (Crane's hand in ink). Typed lower right, "Hart Crane".

C10.   "O Carib Isle!" T.ms., 1p. (black ribbon). NNC

Title: *O CARIB ISLE!*

First line: The tarantula rattling at the lily's foot

Collation: 1 sheet of typing paper. 26.8 x 20.5 cm.

Contents: Typescript, 35 lines in 8 stanzas of varying lengths. Typed lower right, "Hart Crane | (Copy)".

Note: Copy made by Samuel Loveman in 1932. NNC also has carbon copy of typescript.

C11. "The Mango Tree". T.ms., 1p. (black ribbon). PU

Title: THE MANGO TREE

First line: Let them return, saying you blush for the great

Collation: 1 sheet of typing paper. 28 x 21.5 cm.

Date: ca. 1926.

Contents: Early typescript draft, 13 lines, lacking final 5 lines of published version.

C12. "The Mango Tree". T.ms., 1p. (black carbon). TxU

Title: THE MANGO TREE

First line: Let them return, saying you blush for the great

Collation: 1 sheet of typing paper. 28 x 21.5 cm.

Date: ca. 1926.

Contents: Early typescript draft, 13 lines, lacking final 5 lines of published version. Typed lower right, "Hart Crane".

C13. "The Mango Tree". T.ms., 1p. (black carbon). NNC

Title: THE MANGO TREE

First line: Let them return, saying you blush again for the Great Great-

Collation: 1 sheet of typing paper. 26.8 x 20.3 cm. Two punched holes along left margin with gummed reinforcements.

Date: ca. 1926.

Contents: Typescript, 16 lines. Typed lower right, "TRANSITION | Hart Crane | Copy".

C14. "The Mango Tree". T.ms., 1p. (black ribbon). NNC

Title: *THE MANGO TREE*

First line: Let them return, saying you blush again for the great

Collation: 1 sheet of typing paper. 27 x 20.7 cm.

Contents: Typescript, 18 lines. Typed lower right, "Hart Crane | (Copy)". One correction in pencil (probably Samuel Loveman's hand).

Note: Copy made by Samuel Loveman in 1932. NNC also has carbon copy of typescript.

C15. "Island Quarry". T.ms., 1p. (black ribbon). NNC

Title: ISLAND QUARRY

First line: Square sheets — they saw the marble into

Collation: 1 sheet of typing paper. 27 x 20.7 cm.

Contents: Typescript, 2 stanzas of 7 and 8 lines, respectively. Typed lower right, "Hart Crane | (Copy)"; typed lower left, "Transition."

Note: Copy made by Samuel Loveman in 1932. NNC also has carbon copy of typescript. Poem written by Crane ca. 1927.

C16. "The Mermen". A.ms., 1p. (Crane's hand in ink). CtY

Title: *The Mermen*

First line: Buddhas and engines serve as undersea.

Collation: 1 sheet of typing paper. 27.8 x 21.5 cm.

Date: November 1928.

Contents: Holograph manuscript, 15 lines in 4 stanzas. Lower right (Crane's hand in ink), "For Wilbur Underwood | November '28 | Hart Crane".

C17. "The Mermen". T.ms., 1p. (black ribbon). PU

Title: THE MERMEN

First line: Buddhas and engines serve us undersea.

Collation: 1 sheet of typing paper. 28 x 21.5 cm.

Date: ca. 1927.

Contents: Typescript, 15 lines in 4 stanzas. Lower right (Crane's hand in ink), "Greetings and love to Waldo | from Hart | wish you'd write!"

C18. "The Mermen". T.ms., 1p. (black ribbon). NNC

Title: THE MERMEN

First line: Buddhas and engines serve us undersea;

Collation: 1 sheet of ruled notebook paper. 26.7 x 20.4 cm. Two holes punched along left margin with gummed reinforcements.

Date: ca. 1927.

Contents: Typescript, 15 lines in 4 stanzas. Typed lower right, "Hart Crane | copy".

Note: NNC also has carbon copy of typescript with one correction in pencil (probably Samuel Loveman's hand).

C19. "The Mermen". T.ms., 1p. (black ribbon). NNC

Title: THE MERMEN

First line: Buddhas and engines serve us undersea;

Collation: 1 sheet of typing paper. 26.8 x 20.7 cm.

Contents: Typescript, 15 lines in 4 stanzas. Typed lower right, "Hart Crane | (Copy)".

Note: Copy made by Samuel Loveman in 1932. NNC also has carbon copy of typescript.

C20. "The Idiot". T.ms., 1p. (black ribbon). NNC

Title: THE IDIOT

First line: Sheer over to the side,—for see

Collation: 1 sheet of typing paper. 26.7 x 20.5 cm.

Contents: Typescript, 4 stanzas of 4 lines each. Typed lower right, "Hart Crane | (Copy)".

Note: Copy made by Samuel Loveman in 1932. NNC also has carbon copy of typescript. Poem written by Crane ca. August 1926.

C21. "A Name for All". T.ms., 1p. (black ribbon). NNC

Title: A NAME FOR ALL

First line: Moonmoth and grasshopper that flee our page

Collation: 1 sheet of typing paper. 26.7 x 20.5 cm.

Contents: Typescript, 3 stanzas of 4 lines each. Typed lower right, "Hart Crane | (Copy)".

Note: Copy made by Samuel Loveman in 1932. NNC also has carbon copy of typescript. Poem written by Crane ca. 1927.

C22. "Royal Palm". T.ms., 1p. (black ribbon). NNC

Title: ROYAL PALM

First line: Green rustlings, more than regal charities

Collation: 1 sheet of typing paper. 26.5 x 20.5 cm.

Contents: Typescript, 4 stanzas of 4 lines each. Typed lower right, "Hart Crane | (Copy)"; typed lower left, "Transition."

Note: Copy made by Samuel Loveman in 1932. NNC also has carbon copy of typescript. Poem written by Crane ca. 1927.

C23. "The Air Plant". T.ms., 1p. (black carbon). NNC

Title: THE AIR PLANT | *Grand Cayman*

First line: This tuft that thrives on saline nothingness,

Collation: 1 sheet of typing paper. 27.2 x 20.5 cm. Two punched holes along left margin with gummed reinforcements.

Date: ca. July 1927.

Contents: Typescript, 4 stanzas of 4 lines each. Typed lower right, "Hart Crane, | RFD - Patterson, N.Y. | As sent to Criterion | July 16th".

C24. "The Air Plant". T.ms., 1p. (black ribbon). CtY

Title: THE AIR PLANT

First line: This plant that thrives on saline nothingness,

Collation: 1 sheet of typing paper. 27.8 x 21.5 cm.

Date: ca. July 1927.

Contents: Typescript, 4 stanzas of 4 lines each. Typed lower right, "Grand Cayman, West Indies".

C25. "The Air Plant". T.ms., 1p. (black ribbon). NNC

Title: THE AIR PLANT | *Grand Cayman*

First line: This tuft that thrives on saline nothingness,

Collation: 1 sheet of typing paper. 26.8 x 20.5 cm.

Contents: Typescript, 4 stanzas of 4 lines each. Typed lower right, "Hart Crane | (Copy)".

Note: Copy made by Samuel Loveman in 1932. NNC also has carbon copy of typescript.

C26. "Imperator Victus". T.ms., 1p. (black ribbon). ICU

Title: IMPERATOR VICTUS

First lines: Big guns again | No speakee well

Collation: 1 sheet of typing paper. 25.5 x 20 cm.

Date: ca. 1927.

Contents: Typescript, 15 lines in 7 stanzas, as published in *Poetry* (January 1933). Editorial markings and notations throughout.

C27. "Imperator Victus". T.ms., 1p. (black ribbon). NNC

Title: IMPERATOR VICTUS

First lines: Big guns again | No speakee well

Collation: 1 sheet of typing paper. 26.7 x 20.5 cm.

Contents: Typescript, 15 lines in 7 stanzas. Typed lower right, "Hart Crane | (Copy)".

Note: Copy made by Samuel Loveman in 1932. NNC also has carbon copy of typescript.

C28. "The Hurricane". T.ms., 1p. (black ribbon). NNC

Title: THE HURRICANE

First line: Lo, Lord, Thou ridest!

Collation: 1 sheet of white stationery. 22.5 x 14.5 cm. (With envelope addressed to Solomon M. Grunberg and postmarked 26 February 1931.)

Date: 26 February 1931.

Contents: Typescript, 9 stanzas of 2 lines each, text varying in several instances from version published in *transition* (December 1927) and CP. On bottom of sheet is four-line note from Crane to Grunberg.

C29. "The Hurricane". T.ms., 1p. (black ribbon). ICU

Title: THE HURRICANE

First line: Lo, Lord, Thou ridest!

Collation: 1 sheet of typing paper. 21.5 x 19.5 cm.

Date: ca. 1927.

Contents: Typescript, 9 stanzas of 2 lines each. Typed lower right, "Hart Crane".

C30. "The Hurricane". T.ms., 1p. (black ribbon). NNC

Tilte: THE HURRICANE

First line: Lo, Lord, Thou ridest!

Collation: 1 sheet of typing paper. 26.8 x 20.5 cm.

Contents: Typescript, 9 stanzas of 2 lines each. One correction in pencil (Samuel Loveman's hand). Typed lower right, "Hart Crane | (Copy)".

Note: Copy made by Samuel Loveman in 1932. NNC also has carbon copy of typescript.

C31. "Bacardi Spreads the Eagle's Wings". T.ms., 1p. (black ribbon). NNC

Title: BACARDI SPREADS THE EAGLE'S WINGS

First line: Pablo and Pedro, and black Serafin

Collation: 1 sheet of typing paper. 26.8 x 20.5 cm.

Contents: Typescript, 3 stanzas of 4 lines each. Typed lower right, "Hart Crane | (Copy)"; typed lower left, "Transition."

Note: Copy made by Samuel Loveman in 1932. NNC also has carbon copy of typescript. Poem written by Crane ca. 1927.

C32. "And Bees of Paradise". T.ms., 1p. (black ribbon). NNC

Title: AND BEES OF PARADISE

First line: I had come all the way here from the sea,

Collation: 1 sheet of typing paper. 26.8 x 20.5 cm.

Contents: Typescript, 10 lines. Typed lower right, "Hart Crane | (Copy)".

Note: Copy made by Samuel Loveman in 1932. NNC also has carbon copy of typescript. Poem written by Crane ca. 1927.

C33. "To Emily Dickinson". T.ms., 1p. (black ribbon). PU

Title: TO EMILY DICKINSON

First line: You who desired so much—in vain to ask—

Collation: 1 sheet of typing paper. 28 x 21.5 cm. (Typed on top of sheet containing typed letter, with six-line postscript in ink, from Crane to Waldo Frank, 21 November [1926].)

Date: 21 November 1926.

Contents: Late typescript, 3 stanzas of 4 lines and 1 stanza of 2 lines.

C34. "To Emily Dickinson". T.ms., 1p. (black ribbon). ICU

Title: TO EMILY DICKINSON

First line: You who desired so much—in vain to ask—

Collation: 1 sheet of typing paper. 28 x 21.5 cm.

Date: ca. November 1926.

Contents: Late typescript, 3 stanzas of 4 lines each and 1 stanza of 2 lines. Typed lower right, "Hart Crane".

C35. "To Emily Dickinson". T.ms., 1p. (black ribbon). NNC

Title: TO EMILY DICKINSON

First line: You who desired so much—in vain to ask—

Collation: 1 sheet of typing paper. 26.7 x 20.5 cm.

Contents: Typescript, 3 stanzas of 4 lines and 1 stanza of 2 lines. Typed lower right, "Hart Crane | (Copy)"; typed lower left, "Nation- June | 27".

Note: Copy made by Samuel Loveman in 1932. NNC also has carbon copy of typescript.

C36. "Moment Fugue". T.ms., 1p. (black ribbon). NNC

Title: *M O M E N T   F U G U E*

First line: The syphillitic selling violets calmly

Collation: 1 sheet of typing paper. 26.8 x 20.5 cm.

Contents: Typescript, 15 lines in 3 stanzas. Typed lower right, "Hart Crane | (Copy)".

Note: Copy made by Samuel Loveman in 1932. NNC also has carbon copy of typescript. Poem written by Crane ca. 1926.

C37. "To the Cloud Juggler". T.ms., 1p. ICarbS

Title: In Memoriam Harry Crosby [earlier title "Panegyric" canceled]

First line: The sun is cold - his body low,

Date: ca. 1930.

Contents: Probably an early draft.

Note: Citation and description incomplete since manuscript withheld from use.

C38. "To the Cloud Juggler". T.ms., 1p. (black ribbon). NNC

Title: TO | THE CLOUD JUGGLER

First line: What you may cluster 'round the knees of space

Collation: 1 sheet of typing paper. 26.8 x 20.5 cm.

Contents: Typescript, 5 stanzas of 4 lines each. Typed lower right, "Hart Crane | (Copy)".

Note: Copy made by Samuel Loveman in 1932. NNC also has carbon copy of typescript. Poem written by Crane ca. 1930.

C39. "By Nilus Once I Knew". T.ms., 1p. (black ribbon). ICU

Title: BY NILUS ONCE I KNEW [last two words canceled in ink]

First line: Some old Egyptian joke is in the air,

Collation: 1 sheet of typing paper. 25.5 x 20 cm.

Date: ca. 1927.

Contents: Typescript, 4 stanzas of 4 lines each, as published in *Poetry* (January 1933). Editorial markings and notations throughout.

C40. "By Nilus Once I Knew". T.ms., 1p. (black ribbon). NNC

Title: BY NILUS ONCE I KNEW . . .

First line: Some old Egyptian joke is in the air

Collation: 1 sheet of typing paper. 27 x 20.5 cm.

Contents: Typescript, 4 stanzas of 4 lines each. Typed lower right, "Hart Crane | (Copy)".

Note: Copy made by Samuel Loveman in 1932. NNC also has carbon copy of typescript.

C41. "To Shakespeare". T.ms., 1p. (black ribbon). NNC

Title: TO SHAKESPEARE

First line: Through torrid entrances, past icy poles

Collation: 1 sheet of typing paper. 26.8 x 20.5 cm.

Contents: Typescript, sonnet, 14 lines. One correction in pencil (Samuel Loveman's hand). Typed lower right, "Hart Crane | (Copy)". Poem is variant version of "The Tree: Great William" (see item C42).

Note: Copy made by Samuel Loveman in 1932. NNC also has carbon copy of typescript. Poem written by Crane ca. 1927–1930.

C42. "The Tree: Great William". T.ms., 1p. (black ribbon). NNC

Title: THE TREE | GREAT WILLIAM

First line: Through torrid entrances, & by icy poles

Collation: 1 sheet of typing paper. 26.6 x 20.3 cm.

Contents: Typescript, sonnet, 14 lines. Typed lower right, "Hart Crane | (Copy)". Poem is variant version of "To Shakespeare" (see item C41).

Note: Copy made by Samuel Loveman in 1932. NNC also has carbon copy of typescript. Poem written by Crane ca. 1927–1930.

C43. "The Broken Tower". T.ms., 1p. (black ribbon). NNC

Title: THE BROKEN TOWER

First line: The bell cord that gathers God at dawn

Collation: 1 sheet of typing paper. 27.7 x 21.5 cm.

Date: ca. February 1932. (Probably version referred to in letter from Crane to Solomon Grunberg, 8 February 1932, in collection at NNC.)

Contents: Early typescript draft, 4 stanzas of 4 lines each, corresponding to stanzas 1, 2, 3, and 5 in version published in *New Republic* (June 8, 1932) and CP, with several variations in the text. Two corrections in ink (Crane's hand). Beneath last line of text is typed "(More to follow - this is the new beginning)". Signed "Hart", underscored.

C44. "The Broken Tower". T.ms., 1p. (black ribbon). ViU

Title: *THE BROKEN TOWER*

First line: The bell cord that gathers God at dawn

Collation: 1 sheet of typing paper. 27.8 x 21.5 cm.

Date: 9 February 1932.

Contents: Early typescript draft, 4 stanzas of 4 lines each, corresponding to stanzas 1, 2, 3, and 5 in version published in *New Republic* (June 8, 1932) and CP, with several variations in text. Corrections and emendations in ink (Crane's hand). Typed upper right, "Mixcoac, Feb. 9th '32", and lower right, "—To be continued, by | your | Hart", name signed in ink and underscored.

C45. "The Broken Tower". T. and a.ms., 4p. (black ribbon; Crane's hand in ink). ViU

Title: THE BROKEN TOWER

First line: The bell-rope that gathers God at dawn

Collation: 2 sheets of typing paper, written on both sides. 27.8 x 21.5 cm.

Date: 14 March 1932.

Contents: On recto of first sheet, typescript of first 8 stanzas with first 2 lines of stanza 9 (Crane's hand in ink); emendations (Crane's hand in ink), and signed

ILLUSTRATIONS

Frondage of dark islands, breathing
the crocus lustres of the stars--
repeated ease, repeated awe
enclose me with the night that trails

enclose me, aching with the night
that trails its rites from isle to isle.

            VOYAGES - II

Frondage of dark islands, breathing
the crocus lustres of the stars--   *minstrel mansion,*
repeated ease, repeated awe   *~~ease~~*
enclose me, aching with the night   *aching*
that trails its rites from isle to isle.
               red like flediwig
Silhouettes of sceptres roving   *swimming*
flash ~~mark the white~~ shoulders, O sadly
soothing as a vanished lily grove;
and you whose arms dip now in mine,
in turn, you too, immeasurably --
to see your ~~will smile and~~ dive with phantom ease!
         smiling
Bells ringing off San Salvador
~~on~~ scrolls of silver , ivory sentences
brimming confession, O prodigal,
in which your tongue slips mine,--
~~the perfect diapason danced~~

in minstrel mansions

the perfect diapason, dancing leftward's

~~the~~ where in minstrel mansions shine

~~I saw~~

~~the~~ Fervent crosses of the tides,
obey the light that you have seen t
Repeated joy, repeated awe --

And it is ghostly here

columbus will - knowledge

Isabella's will - Christ

Fernande's will - gold

- 3 ships
- 2 destroyed

1 remaining will, Columbus

"-And they who mutinied against her Christ
who gave the jewels-(for whom she offered jewels)
went with his lust for gold, alas!
Fernande, thou!

O sun that pointest Cathay

The Promised Lands, the sphere

riddle

reave   beauty

of sojourn

waring

the watch
wear of the watch

Strong gale & high seas running

made sail

steering by wind

yards braced

stood away on the starboard Tack

Rudder scans the path

Sun that dost point and prove and leant not my argument

Thy sphere that stopped back into the sea

Some testament committed in a cask

to send some back into a ship

the plains of Cordoba into a chest

now   Louis de St Angel now

Be with me, then Fray Juan Perez; for I more the deny
                                    cannot

Has seen what writers would not believe

Be with me now who rode a donkey to the green

Be with us now before the tide sets away

renew my suit   receive the word away

clotted with sumach

buckskin mare	ford
corral	bridle-reins
harness	haunched
footing	leash
snort	tiers
rump	shale

To Samuel Loveman
from Hart Crane
December 31, 1929

Macadam, gun-grey as the tunny's belt
Leaps from Far Rockaway to Golden Gate.
So many mornings, boarding a car for work —

spare hands

daemp tonnage once alluvial might of days
And longer nights that no inch of rock —
The water-smiths length of sand and clays
Red, ocher, lynx-ribbed and final on the shifting floor
The night that promises ground numbed
barred
Also recalls,

The first star, token fire and faith
Aamonishes the pure flight
→ Over de Soto's bones, to New Orleans
(O crucible of blood, the river passes)
Through her more curves the Mississippi leans

Crucible

the wide trencheant Tongued
Spreads in as wide passion, choked and slow,
The mornings birth age serves you work
meets the Gulf tides silently below. — —
The Gratefull of the morning afore you work
that is not labor, is not task, but deed

Horses and swimmers pass
Time not by these engine laws
Oh, give me time at last   Miraculous, and get them known
To pass you   The other reasonings of fire & snow.
                               Miraculous — that you should go
footings   By reasonings of fire and snow.

The oceans minute is
The rivers minute is the far brook's year
A crown of many craters

3   Drafts of portions of "The River" and "Van Winkle"
(Item B15)

vitreous   Laterite
flaked   Spikes
famine   Archipelago   faith
stubble   (belief)

                                                    ─ fidelity

                              my Salient brow)
Here has withdrawn) thrown me
Out of the valley, past the ample crib
to lost to skies that impartial,
Ed beat the skies aloud disown me
As though I had not Adams bone nor rib.
(exper the   ing spine
(Concur ind)   digi   simpl , diff
Oar-plash, and the meteorite's respond response
finite fugue to wrist and bicep. In the moon
Had now I sunk, I hold the entrance to a notice
                                         same
To heaven's and to hell's bitter frugal moon.

            To skies impartial that do not disown me

        the others
Because reap a dead conclusion
Used of presume the same fruit to 8, my time
As locks then conscious in the ages float confusion
And turns the warm bound into sultry stone
Appearing fantasy, reality and sheer aerie claims
A stauncher forge and bellows, now Than over —
Ransack all reasons for the rain

                 5 Worksheet for "Key West" (Item CIX)

Were space is *eres in a idiom (A clause)

An argosy of patience in their gaze

October   Antarctic

Perspective never withers from their eyes;
They keep that docile edict of the Spring
That blends September with the Arctic skies:
These are but cows that see no other thing
Than grass and snow, and their own inner being
Through the rich halo that they do not trouble
To even cast upon the ~~~~~ the seasons fleeing,
Though they should thin and die an last year's stubble,

    are   awkward   foxes ships

And They ~~stationary~~, ponderous and uncoy—...   6
While So we, who press the cider mill regard them—
We, who on ~~anvil~~ acid-bright annoy
Of friendship, ~~with~~ reprisals, retard phlegm—
Watch cycle after cycle break, ~~destroy~~ amend
~~The garment~~ of our love past present mending,
But seldom ~~pierce~~ the path way

    tread   never ending

And to the garment of past grieving sewn

A collar-breadth of gaiter assume

Transcend

As though head ...igious within us were ashamed

... crop of ...

... lines

dispense that sponsal wine

Stevens

KEY WEST

(handwritten top right: ...sticks a solitary branch)

Here has my salient faith now ~~finally~~ thrown me, *(handwritten: coupled)*
Cut of the valley, past the ample crib,
To skies impartial, that do not disown me
As though I had not Adam's spine nor rib. *(handwritten left: Nor claim me, either, as)*

Oar-plash, and the meteorite's ~~dazkxfafzzresponse~~ *(handwritten: white ... arch ... entrance)*
Concur with wrist and bicep. In the moon
That now has sunk, ~~I hold the entrance nonce~~ *(handwritten: black ...)*
To heaven or hades—the same frugal ~~banxxxzz~~ noon. *(handwritten: in equal)*

Because the others reap a dead conclusion,
Need I presume the same fruit of my bone *(handwritten: night's hot)*
As ~~ixadax~~ feeds them towards a ~~sxiffxxxxxixixxxxxigxix~~ confusion
That ~~monkeys~~ ~~apexin~~ split ~~sxtxtxxxzxfxaxxkxxxf~~ *(handwritten: perpetual summer)*
apes ~~record~~ ~~ig~~ ~~px~~ sutures of stone? *(handwritten: the cliff ... in)*

Here tipped by archipelegoes the seasons wear
Scare but ~~aaxkxmgxzxfx~~ antipodes of spring, ~~Look~~
Into my ~~own~~ heart and ~~xxxixx~~ wall the sun, and stare
Into a midnight that their souls can never brook.

(handwritten:)
That, upon the split ruins of sutured stone?

Yes I can wait with you mine
The passage of the termites to the final sand
And I who know this sky, shall bind
It with a faith that knows a ruling hand.

EUCLID AVENUE

To be or not to be--?

maytimes

~~And~~ so to be the denizen appropriate
Or thin, as nations romanized may show
~~Diverse, but dwindles~~ slow...Hexameters
Suspend jockstraps for gangsters while the pil-

Grievously

~~Grim~~ blanches in Plutarch. The angles break
Into the folds of crepe that drape
The broken door. Crouch ~~then, clench.~~

So, then, and clinch

Sweep...
Clean is that cloven word. Creep.
Clasp oblivion as though chance   *flaut*
Could absent all answers ~~for~~ the chosen ~~moment~~.
        now   *from*

Stop as ~~snarz~~ never, never; then

As telegrams continue, write
Your scholarship through broken ribs. All
Answers Euclid; Einstein curves but does not
~~fail~~. No never take the Eucharist nor
Any boulevard no more... I ~~may mumure~~ *resent.*
                you're prevalent, Prevail.

For there are statues, shapes your use
Repeals... Youse use. ~~Youse prevail.~~ Youse
Food once more and souse, like all men under sail.
You guys, my friends; I ~~thought~~ we'd never fail!
        did it   *never*   *whether*
That dirty peacock's pride, once gory God's one glory:
It ~~don't~~ belong any more; no, don't belong
On Euclid Avenue as ~~didn't~~ Wm.
~~Bleak~~ or blacked, ~~whatever~~ 'twas/. What pride we've
Put in blasted pigs. No more. I says...

But I say; what a swell chance boys. No more
Cancers, jealousy, tangents or giblets! ~~By~~ *Death, boys,*
(nor blinkers either) for shots at who knows who
Grabbed--right out o'my mouth that final chew-
(Eat back that sweet restraint that's thrust in view)
Right there on Euclid Avenue.

7   Typescript draft of "Euclid Avenue" (Item D28)

twice by Crane in ink in lower left. On verso of first
sheet, typed in upper right, "15 Michoacan, | Mixcoac,
D F | Mexico | March 14th, 1932" and on bottom of
sheet draft (Crane's hand in ink), of line 3 of stanza 8.
On recto of second sheet, 2 typescript drafts of stanza 9,
one typescript draft of stanza 8, and draft of stanza 10
(Crane's hand in ink); emendations (Crane's hand in
ink). On verso of second sheet (Crane's hand in ink),
title "Virginia" followed by first 4 lines of poem, and on
bottom half of sheet drafts of first 2 lines of stanza 4 and
last 2 lines of stanza 9 of "The Broken Tower".

C46. "The Broken Tower". T.ms., 3p. (black ribbon). ViU

Title: THE BROKEN TOWER

First line: The bell-rope that gathers God at dawn

Collation: 3 sheets of typing paper. 27.8 x 21.5 cm. Last
two sheets both numbered 2.

Date: ca. March 1932.

Contents: Late typescript draft, with emendations in ink
(Crane's hand). On first sheet, first 8 stanzas; on second
sheet, stanza 9 and two drafts of stanza 10; on third
sheet, stanzas 9 and 10.

C47. "The Broken Tower". T.ms., 2p. (black carbon). CtY

Title: THE BROKEN TOWER

First line: The bell-rope that gathers God at dawn

Collation: 2 sheets of typing paper. 27.8 x 21.3 cm.
Second sheet numbered 2.

Date: ca. March 1932.

Contents: Typescript, 10 stanzas of 4 lines each; one
correction in ink (Crane's hand). On bottom half of
page 2 is typed letter, signed, from Crane to Malcolm
Cowley, Easter 1932.

C48. "The Broken Tower". T.ms., 2p. (black ribbon). NNC

Title: THE BROKEN TOWER

First line: The bell-rope that gathers God at dawn

Collation: 2 sheets of onionskin paper. 27.8 x 21.3 cm.
(With envelope postmarked Mixcoac, D. F., 29 March
1932.)

Date: 29 March 1932.

Contents: Typescript, 10 stanzas of 4 lines each, as
published in *New Republic* (June 8, 1932) and CP;
one correction in stanza 6 (Crane's hand in ink). On
p. 2 following text is typed note signed from Crane to
Samuel Loveman.

C49. "The Broken Tower". T.ms., 1p. (black ribbon). NNC

Title: *The Broken Tower*

First line: The bell-rope that gathers God at dawn

Collation: 1 sheet of typing paper. 26.8 x 20.3 cm.

Date: ca. March 1932. (Undoubtedly version referred
to in letters from Crane to Malcolm Cowley and Samuel
Loveman, Easter 1932.)

Contents: Typescript, 10 stanzas of 4 lines each. Typed
lower right, "Hart Crane | (Copy)".

Note: Copy made by Samuel Loveman in 1932. NNC
also has carbon copy of typescript.

C50. "The Phantom Bark". T.ms., 1p. (black ribbon). NNC

Title: fragment note

First line: So dream thy sails, O phantom bark

Collation: 1 sheet of buff onionskin paper. 27.8 x 21.5
cm.

Date: ca. 1926.

Contents: Typescript draft, 3 stanzas of 4 lines each. One alteration and six words in pencil in last line (Crane's hand).

C51. "The Phantom Bark". T.ms., 1p. (black ribbon). ICU

Title: PHANTOM BARK

First line: So dream thy sails, O phantom bark,

Collation: 1 sheet of typing paper. 25.5 x 20 cm.

Date: ca. 1926.

Contents: Typescript, 3 stanzas of 4 lines each, as published in *Poetry* (January 1933). Typed upper left, "fragment note". Editorial markings throughout.

C52. "The Phantom Bark". T.ms., 1p. (black ribbon). NNC

Title: *Phantom Bark* [Samuel Loveman's hand in pencil]

First line: So dream thy sails, O phantom bark

Collation: 1 sheet of typing paper. 27 x 20.5 cm.

Contents: Typescript, 3 stanzas of 4 lines each. Typed upper left, "fragment note"; typed lower right, "Hart Crane | (Copy)".

Note: Copy made by Samuel Loveman in 1932. NNC also has carbon copy of typescript.

C53. "Old Song". T.ms., 1p. (black ribbon). NNC

Title: *OLD SONG*

First line: Thine absence overflows the rose,—

Collation: 1 sheet of typing paper. 27 x 20.7 cm.

Contents: Typescript, 3 stanzas of 4 lines each. Typed lower right, "Hart Crane | (Copy)"; typed lower left, "New Republic—Aug./27."

Note: Copy made by Samuel Loveman in 1932. NNC also has carbon copy of typescript. Poem written by Crane ca. 1927.

D.

MINOR, UNCOLLECTED, AND UNPUBLISHED POEMS

D1. "After Jonah". T.ms., 1p. (black ribbon). TxU

Title: After Jonah

First line: In my beginning was the memory, somehow

Collation: 1 sheet of typing paper. 28 x 21.5 cm.

Date: ca. 1922–1926.

Contents: Typescript of unpublished poem, 4 stanzas, of which first 3 have 4 lines and final stanza 5 lines.

D2. "The alert pillow". A.ms., 1p. (Crane's hand in pencil). NNC

First line: The alert pillow, the hay-seed spreads

Collation: 1 sheet of stationery. 17.5 x 15.3 cm. (Imprinted on verso in blue ink, "Joy Farm | Silver Lake, N. H. | Telephone & Telegraph | Madison, N. H.")

Date: ca. July 1930. (Crane visited E. E. Cummings at Silver Lake, N. H., in July 1930.)

Contents: Draft of untitled poem, 9 lines (Crane's hand in pencil), as published in *"Hart Crane": A Conversation with Samuel Loveman* (New York, Interim Books, 1964). Two emendations (Crane's hand in pencil).

D3. "All this—and the housekeeper". A.ms., 1p. (Crane's hand in pencil). NNC

First line: All this—and the housekeeper—

Collation: 1 sheet of typing paper. 28 x 21.5 cm. (Written on verso of letter from Eugene O'Neill to Crane, 1 March 1926.)

Date: ca. March 1926.

Contents: Draft of unpublished poem, 2 stanzas of 9 lines each (Crane's hand in pencil).

Note: NNC also has typescript copy of poem made by Brom Weber, ca. 1948.

D4. "America's Plutonic Ecstacies". T.ms., 1p. (black ribbon). OU

Title: AMERICA'S PLUTONIC ECSTACIES

First line: Prefering laxatives to wine

Collation: 1 sheet of typing paper. 27.5 x 21.3 cm. (Enclosed in letter from Crane to Gorham B. Munson, 27 January [1923].)

Date: January 1923.

Contents: Typescript, 25 lines in 5 stanzas of varying lengths; one emendation (Crane's hand in ink). Text varies in several instances from ones published in S4N (January 1923) and BW, pp. 390–91. Signed by Crane at end of poem, and with typewritten note following.

D5. "At Heaven Gates". T.ms., 1p. (black ribbon). OU

Title: *AT HEAVEN GATES*

First lines: At length the vermin | and the rod

Collation: 1 sheet of typing paper. 27.7 x 21.5 cm.

Date: 17 October 1924.

Contents: Typescript of unpublished poem, 18 lines in 4 stanzas of varying lengths. Typed note from Crane to Gorham B. Munson, 17 October 1924, on bottom of sheet. Portions of poem were later revised into stanza 5 of "Lachrymae Christi".

D6. "At Heaven Gates". T.ms., 1p. (black ribbon). PU

Title: *AT HEAVEN GATES*

First lines: At length the vermin | and the rod

Collation: 1 sheet of typing paper. 28 x 21.5 cm.

Date: 22 October 1924.

Contents: Typescript of unpublished poem, 19 lines in 4 stanzas of varying lengths. Lower right (Crane's hand in ink), "Dear Waldo— | This poem is, somehow, dedicated | to you, who will understand. | Hart | 10/22/24".

D7. "Belle Isle". T.ms., 1p. (black ribbon). OU

Title: BELLE ISLE

First line: There was the river;—now there is

Collation: 1 sheet of typing paper. 27.7 x 21.5 cm. (Enclosed in letter from Crane to Gorham B. Munson, ca. January 1923.)

Date: ca. January 1923.

Contents: Typescript, 6 stanzas of 4 lines each, as published in BW, p. 391. Poem later revised to form "Voyages VI" (see item A51). Typed note by Crane on bottom of sheet.

D8. "Belle Isle". T.ms., 1p. (black ribbon). PU

Title: BELLE ISLE

First line: There was the river;— now there is

Collation: 1 sheet of typing paper. 28 x 21.5 cm.

Date: ca. January 1923.

Contents: Typescript, 6 stanzas of 4 lines each, as published in BW, p. 391.

D9. "The Bridge of Estador". T.ms., 1p. (black carbon). NNC

Title: THE BRIDGE OF ESTADOR

First line: Walk high on the bridge of Estador,

Collation: 1 sheet of typing paper. 28.2 x 21.5 cm.

Date: ca. April 1921.

Contents: Carbon copy typescript, 4 stanzas of 8, 7, 6, and 10 lines, respectively, varying from version published in BW, p. 385.

D10. "The Bridge of Estador". T.ms., 2p. (black ribbon). OU

Title: THE BRIDGE OF ESTADOR | &&&& | An Impromptu, | Aesthetic | TIRADE | by | Hart Crane [typed on first page of folded sheet; above title is pen-and-ink sketch of a cage]

First line: Walk high on the bridge of Estador,

Collation: 1 sheet of typing paper folded in half. Size of full sheet, 27 x 21.5 cm. (Enclosed in letter from Crane to Gorham B. Munson, 10 April [1921].)

Date: 10 April 1921.

Contents: Typescript, 32 lines in 6 stanzas of varying lengths, as published in BW, p. 385.

D11. "The Circumstance". A.ms., 1p. (Crane's hand in pencil). NNC

First lines: The annointed stones— | the drastic thrones

Collation: 1 sheet of tan notebook paper. 19.5 x 13 cm.

Date: ca. 1931.

Contents: Draft of first stanza and beginning portion of second stanza, 9 lines (Crane's hand in pencil).

D12. "The Circumstance". T.ms., 1p. (black ribbon). NNC

First lines: The annointed stone | The drastic throne

Collation: 1 sheet of typing paper. 27.7 x 21.5 cm.

Date: ca. March-April 1932.

Contents: Typescript draft, 17 lines, with 2 additional lines in ink (Crane's hand); emendations and corrections (Crane's hand in ink). Written on bottom half of sheet of typewritten "Memoranda" relating to debts and transportation indicating that draft was made shortly before Crane left Mixcoac in April 1932.

D13. "The Circumstance". T.ms., 1p. (black ribbon). NNC

Title: THE CIRCUMSTANCE | *To Xochipilli*

First lines: The annointed stone, | The drastic throne

Collation: 1 sheet of tan typing paper. 28 x 21.5 cm.

Date: ca. March-April 1932.

Contents: Late typescript draft, 24 lines in 3 stanzas of 5, 12, and 7 lines, respectively; emendations and corrections (Crane's hand in ink). Top center, "2", encircled in pencil.

D14. "The Circumstance". T.ms., 1p. (black ribbon). ICU

Title: THE CIRCUMSTANCE

First line: The anointed stone, the coruscated crown,

Collation: 1 sheet of typing paper. 25.5 x 20 cm.

Date: ca. March-April 1932.

Contents: Typescript, 3 stanzas of 5, 12, and 7 lines, respectively, as published in *Poetry* (January 1933). Editorial markings throughout.

D15. "The Circumstance". T.ms., 1p. (black ribbon). NNC

Title: THE CIRCUMSTANCE | *To Xochipilli*

First line: The anointed stone, the coruscated crown

Collation: 1 sheet of typing paper. 26.7 x 20.5 cm.

Contents: Typescript, 3 stanzas of 5, 12, and 7 lines, respectively; several corrections in pencil (Samuel Loveman's hand). Typed lower right, "HART CRANE | (Copy)".

Note: Copy made by Samuel Loveman in 1932. NNC also has carbon copy of typescript.

D16. "Dust now is the old-fashioned house". T. and a.ms., 2p. (black ribbon; Crane's hand in pencil). NNC

First line: Dust now is the old-fashioned house

Collation: 1 sheet of tan notebook paper, torn along the top edge and written on both sides. 11 x 14.5 cm.

Date: ca. 1920.

Contents: On recto, two unpublished typewritten drafts of one 4-line stanza; two emendations (Crane's hand in pencil). On verso, 5 lines (Crane's hand in pencil), beginning "There are the local orchard boughs" and related to poem "Garden Abstract".

D17. "Echoes". T.ms., 1p. (black ribbon). NNC

Title: ECHOES

First line: Slivvers of rain upon the pain,

Collation: 1 sheet of typing paper. 28 x 21.5 cm. (Enclosed in letter from Crane to the Rev. Mr. Charles C. Bubb, 13 November 1918.)

Date: ca. 1917–1918.

Contents: Typescript, 3 stanzas of 4 lines each, as published in SL. Version differs in several instances from one published in BW, pp. 381–82. Lower right in pencil, "Bubb E", encircled (unknown hand).

D18. "Enrich My Resignation". T.ms., 1p. (black ribbon). NNC

Title: Enrich my resignation

First line: Enrich my reisgnation as I usurp those those far

Collation: 1 sheet of typing paper. 27.5 x 21.4 cm.

Date: ca. 1923–1926.

Contents: Typescript draft, 11 lines, last 5 lines canceled in pencil; emendations (Crane's hand in ink). Upper right, "Marks | Bryant 3988" (Crane's hand in ink). Top center, "7", in pencil (probably Samuel Loveman's hand).

D19. "Enrich My Resignation". T.ms., 1p. (black ribbon). NNC

Title: Enrich My Resignation [Samuel Loveman's hand in pencil, written above typed title, "The Release", canceled in pencil]

First line: Enrich my resignation as I usurp those far

Collation: 1 sheet of typing paper. 26.8 x 20.5 cm.

Contents: Typescript, 2 stanzas of 6 and 5 lines, respectively; several notations and corrections (Samuel Love-

man's hand in pencil). Typed lower right, "HART
CRANE | (Copy)". Center top, "7", in pencil.

Note: Copy made by Samuel Loveman in 1932. NNC
also has carbon copy of typescript.

D20. "Enrich My Resignation". T.ms., 1p. (black ribbon).
ICU

Title: ENRICH MY RESIGNATION

First line: Enrich my resignation as I usurp those far

Collation: 1 sheet of typing paper. 25.5 x 20 cm.

Date: ca. 1923–1926.

Contents: Typescript as published in *Poetry* (January
1933). Editorial markings and notations throughout.

D21. "Episode of Hands". T.ms., 1p. (black ribbon). OU

Title: EPISODE OF HANDS

First line: The unexpected interest made him flush.

Collation: 1 sheet of typing paper. 26.7 x 18 cm. (Enclosed in letter from Crane to Gorham B. Munson, 26
April 1920.)

Date: 26 April 1920.

Contents: Typescript, 24 lines in 5 stanzas of varying
lengths, as published in BW, p. 384.

D22. "'Ere midnight sifts away another day". A.ms., 1p.
(Crane's hand in ink). NNC

First line: 'Ere midnight sifts away another day

Collation: 1 sheet of ruled notebook paper. 26.5 x 20.2
cm. Four punched holes along left margin. Lower left
corner torn away.

Date: ca. 1915–1916.

Contents: Draft of unpublished sonnet (Crane's hand in ink).

D23. "Ere elfish Night shall sift another day". T.ms., 1p. (purple ribbon). NNC

Title: SONNET

First line: Ere elfish Night shall sift another day

Collation: 1 sheet of stationery. 25.3 x 19.8 cm.

Date: ca. 1915–1916.

Contents: Typescript of unpublished sonnet differing in text from sonnet described in item D22. Written in ink across top of sheet, "An Early Poem of Hart Crane. Samuel Loveman".

D24. "Eternity". T.ms., 2p. (black ribbon). NNC

Title: E T E R N I T Y

First line: After it was over, though still gusting balefully,

Collation: 2 sheets of typing paper. 27.8 x 21.5 cm. Second sheet numbered 2.

Date: ca. 1926–1927.

Contents: Typescrpit, 60 lines in 7 stanzas of varying lengths. One correction on p. 2 (Crane's hand in ink). Typed on p. 2 lower right, "Hart Crane, | RFD - Patterson, N.Y." Typed on p. 2 upper left, "Eternity -2".

D25. "Euclid Avenue". T.ms., 1p. (black ribbon). NNC

Title: E U C L I D   A V E N U E

First line: And so to be the denizen, appropriate

Collation: 1 sheet of typing paper. 27.8 x 21.5 cm.

Date: ca. February 1923.

Contents: Typescript draft, 30 lines in 8 stanzas of varying lengths; emendations (Crane's hand in ink). Upper
left, "#1" (unknown hand in pencil.)

D26. "Euclid Avenue". T.ms., 1p. (black ribbon). NNC

Title: *Euclid Avenue*

First line: And so — to be the denizen, appropriate

Collation: 1 sheet of onionskin paper. 28 x 21.2 cm.

Date: ca. February 1923.

Contents: Typescript draft, 25 lines in 6 stanzas of
varying lengths; emendations (Crane's hand in ink).
Upper left, "#2" (unknown hand in pencil).

D27. "Euclid Avenue". T.ms., 1p. (black ribbon). NNC

Title: *EUCLID AVENUE*

First line: But so to be the denizen appropriate

Collation: 1 sheet of onionskin paper. 28.8 x 21.2 cm.

Date: ca. February 1923.

Contents: Typescript draft, 34 lines in 10 stanzas of
varying lengths; emendations (Crane's hand in ink).
Signed in ink by Crane, lower right. Upper left, "#2"
(unknown hand in pencil).

D28. "Euclid Avenue". T.ms., 2p. (black ribbon). NNC

Title: *EUCLID AVENUE*

First line: But so to be the denizen appropriate

Collation: 1 sheet of typing paper, written on both sides. 27.2 x 20.7 cm.

Date: ca. February 1923. (However, fragment of review on verso is of volume published in 1931.)

Contents: On recto, typescript draft, 32 lines in 9 stanzas of varying lengths, with emendations (Crane's hand in ink); upper left, "#3" (unknown hand in pencil). On verso, typescript draft of portion of review of Howard Phelps Putnam's *The Five Seasons* (see items E8), with corrections and emendations (Crane's hand in pencil). (See Fig. 7.)

D29. "Euclid Avenue". T.ms., 1p. (black ribbon). NNC

Title: EUCLID AVENUE

First line: But so to be the denizen stingaree—

Collation: 1 sheet of onionskin paper. 28 x 21.5 cm.

Date: ca. February 1923.

Contents: Late typescript draft, 34 lines in 12 stanzas of varying lengths, as published in BW, pp. 392–93; notations and emendations (Crane's hand in pencil). Upper left, "final | Hart | 4 A.M.", Crane's hand in pencil. Upper left, "#4" (unknown hand in pencil).

D30. "Euclid Avenue". T.ms., 1p. (black ribbon). PU

Title: EUCLID AVENUE

First line: But so to be the denizen stingaree—

Collation: 1 sheet of typing paper. 28 x 21.5 cm.

Date: ca. February 1923.

Contents: Late typescript draft, 35 lines in 12 stanzas of varying lengths, as published in BW, pp. 392–93. Typed lower right, "HART CRANE".

D31. "Euclid Avenue". T.ms., 1p. (black ribbon). NNC

Title: EUCLID AVENUE

First line: But so to be the denizen stingaree—

Collation: 1 sheet of typing paper. 26.7 x 20.5 cm.

Contents: Typescript, 35 lines in 12 stanzas of varying lengths, as published in BW, pp. 392–93; corrections in pencil (Samuel Loveman's hand). Typed lower right, "HART CRANE | (Copy)".

Note: Copy made by Samuel Loveman in 1932. NNC also has two carbon copies of typescript.

D32. "Exile". T.ms., 1p. (black ribbon). NNC

Title: EXILE | (after the Chinese)

First line: My hands have not touched pleasure since your hands,-

Collation: 1 sheet of typing paper. 28 x 21.5 cm. (Enclosed in letter from Crane to the Rev. Mr. Charles C. Bubb, 13 November 1918.)

Date: ca. 1917–1918.

Contents: Typescript, 2 stanzas of 4 lines each, as published in SL. Lower right in pencil, "Bubb B", encircled (unknown hand).

D33. "Havana Rose". A.ms., 2p. (Crane's hand in ink). NNC

Title: HAVANA ROSE [Crane's hand in ink]

First line: Let us strip the desk for action—now we have a house

Collation: 2 sheets of typing paper. 27.3 x 21 cm.

Date: ca. 1931.

Contents: Draft of prose poem; emendations (Crane's hand in ink).

D34. "Havana Rose". T.ms., 1p. (black ribbon). NNC

Title: *H AV AN A R O S E*

First line: Let us strip the desk for action—now we have a house

Collation: 1 sheet of typing paper. 26.8 x 20.5 cm.

Contents: Typescript, with several corrections and notations (Samuel Loveman's hand in pencil). Center top, "4", in pencil.

Note: Copy made by Samuel Loveman in 1932. NNC also has carbon copy of typescript.

D35. "Havana Rose". T.ms., 1p. (black ribbon). ICU

Title: *H AV AN A R O S E*

First line: Let us strip the desk for action—now we have a house

Collation: 1 sheet of typing paper. 25.5 x 20 cm.

Date: ca. 1931.

Contents: Typescript as published in *Poetry* (January 1933). Editorial markings and notations throughout.

D36. "Her eyes had the blue of desperate days". A.ms., 2p. (Crane's hand in pencil). NNC

First line: Her eyes had the blue of desperate days

Collation: 2 sheets of light-green typing paper. 28 x 21.5 cm. (Written on verso of carbon copy of letter from Crane to Thomas Selzer, 4 May 1925.)

Date: ca. May 1925.

Contents: On verso of p. 2 of letter are 11 unpublished lines (Crane's hand in pencil); on verso of p. 1 are 2 lines (Crane's hand in pencil), "I heard the breath of Holofernes twist | Judith's cold bosom through her righteous years".

Note: NNC also has typescript copy of fragments made by Brom Weber on March 9, 1949.

D37. "Hieroglyphic". T. and a.ms., 1p. (black ribbon; Crane's hand in red pencil). NNC

Title: HIEROGLYPHIC

First line: Did one look at what one saw

Collation: 1 sheet of typing paper. 27.5 x 21.5 cm. (Written on verso of letter from Crane to Irita Van Doren from Mixcoac, Mexico, ca. 1931–1932.)

Date: ca. 1931–1932.

Contents: Typescript of unpublished 2-line fragment, first ten words written a second time in red pencil at bottom of sheet; "Did one look at what one saw | Or did one see what one looked at?"

D38. "I have that sure enclitic to my act". A.ms., 2p. (Crane's hand in ink). NNC

First line: I have that sure enclitic to my act

Collation: Envelope, written on both sides. 24 x 10.7 cm.

Date: ca. 1926–1929.

Contents: Unpublished fragment, 3 lines on recto and 5 lines on verso (Crane's hand in ink).

D39. "I rob my bread to reach those altitudes". A.ms., 2p. (Crane's hand in ink). NNC

First line: I rob my bread to reach those altitudes

Collation: 1 sheet of typing paper, written on both sides. 27.5 x 21.3 cm.

Date: ca. 1928–1930.

Contents: Unpublished fragment (Crane's hand in ink), 13 lines on recto and 4 lines on verso.

D40. "In the Shadow of the Sun". T.ms., 1p. ICarbS

First line: I saw a moment in your face

Collation: 1 sheet of typing paper.

Date: February 28, 1932.

Note: Citation and description incomplete because manuscript withheld from use.

D41. "Interludium". T.ms., 1p. (black ribbon). OU

Title: I N T E R L U D I U M

First line: Thy time is thee to wend

Collation: 1 sheet of tan typing paper. 28 x 21.5 cm.

Date: ca. October 1923.

Contents: Early typescript, 5 stanzas, as published in BW, p. 394.

D42. "Interludium". T.ms., 1p. (black ribbon). NNC

Title: INTERLUDIUM

First line: Thy time is thee to wend

Collation: 1 sheet of typing paper. 27.8 x 21 cm.

Date: ca. January 1924. (See letter from Crane to Isabel and Gaston Lachaise, 9 January 1924, LHC, p. 166.)

Contents: Typescript, 5 stanzas of 4 lines each, as published in BW, pp. 393–94.

D43. "Lenses". T.ms., 1p. (black ribbon). NNC

Title: L E N S E S

First line: In the focus of the evening there is this island with

Collation: 1 sheet of tan onionskin paper. 27.8 x 21.5 cm.

Date: ca. August 1926. (Probably written at same time as "The Idiot".)

Contents: Typescript, 29 lines, as published in BW, p. 396. Typed above title, "(directly preceding Tunnel) | VII or VIII". Entire text canceled in blue ink.

D44. "Love and a Lamp". T.ms., 1p. (black ribbon). NNC

Title: LOVE AND A LAMP

First line: It is a shy solemnity,

Collation: 1 sheet of typing paper. 28 x 21.5 cm. (Enclosed in letter from Crane to the Rev. Mr. Charles C. Bubb, 13 November 1918.)

Date: ca. 1917–1918.

Contents: Typescript, 3 stanzas of 4 lines each, as published in SL. Lower right in pencil, "Bubb D", encircled (unknown hand).

D45. "The Masters". T.ms., 1p. (black ribbon). NNC

Title: fragment note for 'The Masters'

First line: Their brains are smooth machines that colonize

Collation: 1 sheet of tan typing paper. 27.8 x 21.5 cm.

Date: ca. 1926.

Contents: Typescript, 8 lines, as published in BW, p. 399.

D46. "The Masters". T.ms., 1p. (black ribbon). NNC

Title: fragment note - for | THE MASTERS [first line in pencil, Samuel Loveman's hand]

First line: Their brains are smooth machines that colonize

Collation: 1 sheet of typing paper. 26.7 x 20.3 cm.

Contents: Typescript, 8 lines, as published in BW, p. 399. Typed lower right, "HART CRANE | (Copy)".

Note: Copy made by Samuel Loveman in 1932. NNC also has carbon copy of typescript.

D47. "Meditation". T.ms., 1p. (black ribbon). NNC

Title: MEDITATION

First line: I have drawn my hands away

Collation: 1 sheet of typing paper. 28 x 21.5 cm. (Enclosed in letter from Crane to the Rev. Mr. Charles C. Bubb, 13 November 1918.)

Date: ca. 1917–1918.

Contents: Typescript, 3 stanzas of 6 lines each, as published in SL. Lower right in pencil, "Bubb G", encircled (unknown hand).

D48. "Medusa". T.ms., 1p. (black ribbon). NNC

Title: MEDUSA

First lines: Fall with me | Through the frigid stars:

Collation: 1 sheet of typing paper. 28 x 21.5 cm. (Enclosed in letter from Crane to the Rev. Mr. Charles C. Bubb, 13 November 1918.)

Date: ca. 1917–1918.

Contents: Typescript, 3 stanzas of 7, 5, and 2 lines, respectively, as published in SL. Lower right in pencil, "Bubb F", encircled (unknown hand).

D49. "The Moth that God Made Blind". T.ms., 3p. (black ribbon). NNC

Title: THE MOTH THAT GOD MADE BLIND

First line: Among cocoa-nut palms of a far oasis,

Collation: 3 sheets of tan typing paper. 26.4 x 20.2 cm. Last two sheets numbered 2 and 3 in ink, upper left.

Date: 1915.

Contents: Typescript, 13 stanzas of 4 lines each, as published in *Columbia Library Columns* (November 1960); corrections and emendations (Crane's hand in ink). Page 3 lower right (Crane's hand in ink), "(Harold) Hart Crane | 25 E. 11 St. | N.Y.C. | 1915".

D50. "Naiad of Memory". T.ms., 1p. (black ribbon). NNC

Title: NAIAD OF MEMORY

First line: The tossing loneliness of many nights

Collation: 1 sheet of typing paper. 28 x 21.5 cm. (Enclosed in letter from Crane to the Rev. Mr. Charles C. Bubb, 13 November 1918.)

Date: ca. 1917–1918.

Contents: Typescript, 2 stanzas of 5 and 6 lines, as published in SL. Earlier version of "Legende" (see BW, pp. 46–47, 383–84). Lower right in pencil, "Bubb C", encircled (unknown hand).

D51. "O moon, thou sibilance of the sun". A. and t.ms., 1p. (Crane's hand in ink; black ribbon). PU

First line: O moon, thou sibilance of the sun, we utmost love

Collation: 1 sheet of typing paper. 27.8 x 21.5 cm.

Date: ca. 1927–1929.

Contents: Draft of unpublished fragment, 12 lines, of which 8 are in manuscript (Crane's hand) and 4 are typewritten.

D52. "Oyster". T.ms., 1p. (black ribbon). NNC

First line: Time cannot be worn strapped to the wrist

Collation: 1 sheet of typing paper. 27.5 x 21.3 cm.

Date: ca. 1923–1925.

Contents: Early typescript draft, 5 lines; emendations (Crane's hand in ink). Upper left, "liquidate the schedule", and lower left, "Warner and Swasey | The Austin Company" (Crane's hand in ink).

D53. "Oyster". A.ms., 1p. (Crane's hand in ink). NNC

Title: Oyster [Crane's hand in ink]

First line: Time is not to be worn, strapped to the wrist,

Collation: 1 sheet of typing paper. 27.5 x 21.5 cm.

Date: ca. 1923–1925.

Contents: Handwritten draft, 2 stanzas of 4 and 3 lines, as published in BW, p. 400; emendations (Crane's hand in ink). Top center, "12", in pencil (probably Samuel Loveman's hand).

D54. "Oyster". T.ms., 1p. (black ribbon). NNC

Title: OYSTER

First line: Time is not to be worn, strapped to the wrist,

Collation: 1 sheet of typing paper. 26.7 x 20.5 cm.

Contents: Typescript, 2 stanzas of 4 and 3 lines, as published in BW, p. 400. Typed lower right, "HART CRANE | (Copy)". Top center, "12", in pencil (probably Samuel Loveman's hand).

Note: Copy made by Samuel Loveman in 1932. NNC
also has carbon copy of typescript.

D55. "A Persuasion". T.ms., 1p. (black ribbon). OU

Title: A PERSUASION

First line: If she waits late at night

Collation: 1 sheet of typing paper. 28 x 21.5 cm. (Enclosed in letter from Crane to Gorham B. Munson, 16
May 1921.)

Date: 16 May 1921.

Contents: Typescript, 3 stanzas of 4 lines each, as published in BW, pp. 387–88.

D56. "The Pillar and the Post". A.ms., 1p. (Crane's hand in
ink). NNC

Title: *The Pillar and the Post*

First line: What you may yank up readiest Yank—

Collation: 1 sheet of typing paper. 27.3 x 21 cm.

Date: ca. 1926–1927.

Contents: Handwritten draft, 2 stanzas of 5 and 7 lines,
as published in BW, p. 398, with one variation in text.

D57. "The Pillar and the Post". T.ms., 1p. (black ribbon).
NNC

Title: THE PILLAR AND THE POST

First line: What you may yank up readiest, Yank—

Collation: 1 sheet of typing paper. 26.7 x 20.3 cm.

Date: ca. 1926–1927.

Contents: Typescript, 2 stanzas of 5 and 6 lines, as published in BW, p. 398, with one variation in text. Several notations, and upper right, "impossibly confused"

(Samuel Loveman's hand in pencil). Typed lower right, "Hart Crane | (Copy)".

Note: Copy made by Samuel Loveman in 1932. NNC also has two carbon copies of typescript.

D58. "A Placement". T.ms., 1p. (black ribbon). NNC

First line: Shall I subsume the shadow of the world—

Collation: 1 sheet of yellow typing paper. 27.8 x 21.5 cm.

Date: ca. 1923–1925.

Contents: Typescript draft, 2 stanzas of 8 and 5 lines, as published in BW, pp. 399–400. One marking in ink and another in pencil (probably Crane's hand). Top center, "9" in pencil.

D59. "A Placement". T.ms., 1p. (black ribbon). NNC

Title: A PLACEMENT

First line: Shall I subsume the shadow of the world—

Collation: 1 sheet of typing paper. 26.7 x 20.5 cm.

Contents: Typescript, 2 stanzas of 8 and 5 lines, as published in BW, pp. 399–400. Several notations and the last line canceled in pencil (Samuel Loveman's hand). Typed lower right, "HART CRANE | (Copy)". Top center, "9" in pencil.

Note: Copy made by Samuel Loveman in 1932. NNC also has carbon copy of typescript.

D60. "Porphyro in Akron". T.ms., 1p. (black ribbon). OU

First line: A shift of rubber workers presses down South Main

Collation: 1 sheet of typing paper. 25.3 x 20.5 cm. (Enclosed in letter from Crane to Gorham B. Munson, 8 June 1920.)

Date: 8 June 1920.

Contents: Early typescript draft of various portions as published in BW, pp. 89–90.

D61. "Porphyro in Akron". T.ms., 1p. (black ribbon). OU

First line: Tumult of weariness from a basement cabaret

Collation: 1 sheet of typing paper. 26.7 x 20.2 cm. Four holes punched along left margin. (Enclosed in letter from Crane to Gorham B. Munson, 18 August 1920.)

Date: 18 August 1920.

Contents: Typescript drafts of final portion as published in BW, pp. 91–92.

D62. "A Postscript". T.ms., 1p. (black ribbon). NNC

Title: A POSTSCRIPT

First line: Friendship agony! words came to me

Collation: 1 sheet of typing paper. 28 x 21.5 cm.

Date: ca. 1926–1928.

Contents: Typescript draft, 3 stanzas of 6, 5, and 5 lines, respectively; emendations and final line (Crane's hand in ink). Top center, "5" in pencil.

D63. "A Postscript". T.ms., 1p. (black ribbon). NNC

Title: A POSTSCRIPT

First line: Friendship agony! words came to me

Collation: 1 sheet of typing paper. 26.8 x 20.5 cm.

Contents: Typescript, 3 stanzas of 6, 5, and 5 lines, respectively. Top center, "5", and one correction in text (Samuel Loveman's hand in pencil). Typed lower right, "HART CRANE | (Copy)".

Note: Copy made by Samuel Loveman in 1932. NNC also has carbon copy of typescript.

D64. "A Postscript". T.ms., 1p. (black ribbon). ICU

Title: A POSTSCRIPT

First line: Friendship agony! words came to me

Collation: 1 sheet of typing paper. 25.5 x 20 cm.

Date: ca. 1926–1928.

Contents: Typescript as published in *Poetry* (January 1933). Editorial markings and notations throughout.

D65. "Purgatorio". A.ms., 2p. (Crane's hand in ink). NNC

Title: *Purgatorio*

First line: My country, O my land, my friends

Collation: 2 sheets of typing paper. 27.8 x 21 cm.

Date: ca. 1930–1931.

Contents: Handwritten draft, 2 stanzas of 13 and 8 lines, respectively (Crane's hand in ink). Additional notes in Crane's hand on bottom half of second sheet. There are minor variations between this version and one published in *Poetry* (January 1933) and CP.

D66. "Purgatorio". A.ms., 2p. (Grace Hart Crane's hand in pencil). NNC

Title: *Purgatorio*

First line: My country, O my land, my friends—

Collation: 1 sheet of typing paper, written on both sides. 27.8 x 21.5 cm.

Date: ca. 1930–1931.

Contents: Handwritten copy by Grace Hart Crane. Upper right, "This is all I could translate of this". Typed on verso and canceled in pencil, "The Carleton, | Oak Park, Ill., | May 28/32".

D67. "Purgatorio". T.ms., 1p. (black ribbon). NNC

Title: *PURGATORIO*

First line: My country, O my land, my friends—

Collation: 1 sheet of typing paper. 26.7 x 20.3 cm.

Contents: Typescript, 2 stanzas of 13 and 8 lines, as published in *Poetry* (January 1933) and CP; corrections and notations (Samuel Loveman's hand in pencil).

Note: Copy made by Samuel Loveman in 1932. NNC also has carbon copy of typescript.

D68. "Purgatorio". T.ms., 1p. (black ribbon). ICU

Title: PURGATORIO

First line: My country, O my land, my friends—

Collation: 1 sheet of typing paper. 25.5 x 20 cm.

Date: ca. 1930–1931.

Contents: Typescript, 2 stanzas of 13 and 8 lines, as published in *Poetry* (January 1933). Editorial markings throughout.

D69. "Reliquary". A.ms., 1p. (Crane's hand in ink). NNC

First lines: Tenderness and resolution | What is our life without a sudden pillow—

Collation: 1 sheet of typing paper. 27.8 x 21.5 cm.

Date: ca. 1929–1932.

Contents: Handwritten draft, 17 lines, as published in *Poetry* (January 1933) and CP; emendations (Crane's hand in ink). Center top, "15" in pencil.

D70. "Reliquary". T.ms., 1p. (black ribbon). NNC

Title: RELIQUARY

First line: Tenderness and resolution!

Collation: 1 sheet of typing paper. 26.7 x 20.3 cm.

Contents: Typescript, 3 stanzas of 3, 10, and 4 lines, as published in *Poetry* (January 1933) and CP; corrections (Samuel Loveman's hand in pencil). Typed lower right, "Hart Crane | (copy)".

Note: Copy made by Samuel Loveman in 1932. NNC also has carbon copy of typescript.

D71. "Reliquary". T.ms., 1p. (black ribbon). ICU

Title: RELIQUARY

First line: Tenderness and resolution!

Collation: 1 sheet of typing paper. 25.5 x 20 cm.

Date: ca. 1929–1932.

Contents: Typescript as published in *Poetry* (January 1933). Editorial markings and notations throughout.

D72. "Reply". T.ms., 1p. (black ribbon). NNC

First line: Thou canst read nothing except through appetite

Collation: 1 sheet of typing paper, lower left corner torn away. 27.8 x 21.6 cm.

Date: ca. 1926–1928.

Contents: Typescript, 3 stanzas of 4 lines each, as published in *Poetry* (January 1933) and CP. Note in Samuel Loveman's hand unrelated to the poem, lower right. Top center, "8" in pencil (Samuel Loveman's hand).

D73. "Reply". T.ms., 1p. (black ribbon). NNC

Title: Reply [Samuel Loveman's hand in pencil; "A PORTRAIT" typed beneath and canceled in pencil]

First line: Thou canst read nothing except through appetite

Collation: 1 sheet of typing paper. 26.7 x 20.4 cm.

Contents: Typescript, 3 stanzas of 4 lines each, as published in *Poetry* (January 1933) and CP. One notation and one correction (Samuel Loveman's hand in pencil). Typed lower right, "HART CRANE | (Copy)".

Note: Copy made by Samuel Loveman in 1932. NNC also has carbon copy of typescript.

D74. "Reply". T.ms., 1p. (black ribbon). ICU

Title: REPLY

First line: Thou canst read nothing except through appetite,

Collation: 1 sheet of typing paper. 25.5 x 20 cm.

Date: ca. 1926–1928.

Contents: Typescript, 3 stanzas of 4 lines each, as published in *Poetry* (January 1933). Editorial markings throughout.

D75. "The Return". T.ms., 1p. (black ribbon). NNC

First line: The sea raised up a campanile; the wind I hear,

Collation: 1 sheet of typing paper. 27.5 x 21.5 cm.

Date: ca. 1926–1928.

Contents: Four typescript drafts totaling 15 lines, final draft on sheet being one published in *New Republic* (February 15, 1933) and CP; emendations (Crane's hand in ink).

D76. "The Return". T.ms., 1p. (black ribbon). NNC

First line: The sea raised up a campanile . . . The wind I heard

Collation: 1 sheet of typing paper. 27.8 x 21.5 cm.

Date: ca. 1926–1928.

Contents: Early typescript draft, 4 lines, text varying from version published in *New Republic* and CP. Top center, "13" in pencil (Samuel Loveman's hand).

D77. "The Return". T.ms., 1p. (black ribbon). NNC

Title: THE RETURN

First line: The sea raised up a campanile . . . The wind I heard

Collation: 1 sheet of typing paper. 26.8 x 20.5 cm.

Contents: Typescript, 4 lines, varying from text published in *New Republic* and CP. Top right, "(earlier version)" (Samuel Loveman's hand in pencil). Typed lower right, "HART CRANE | (Copy)".

Note: Copy made by Samuel Loveman in 1932. NNC also has carbon copy of typescript.

D78. "The Return". T.ms., 1p. (black ribbon). NNC

Title: THE RETURN

First line: The sea raised up a campanile . . . The wind I heard

Collation: 1 sheet of typing paper. 26.8 x 20.5 cm.

Contents: Typescript, 4 lines, as published in *New Republic* and CP. Top center, "13 . . . (last poem in volume)" (Samuel Loveman's hand in pencil); lower right, "best version" (unknown hand in pencil). Typed lower right, "HART CRANE | (Copy)".

Note: Copy made by Samuel Loveman in 1932. NNC also has carbon copy of typescript.

D79. "The Sad Indian". A.ms., 1p. (Crane's hand in ink). NNC

Title: *The Sad Indian*

First line: Sad heart, the gymnast of inertia, does not count

Collation: 1 sheet of ruled paper. 23 x 15.5 cm.

Date: ca. 1930–1931.

Contents: Handwritten draft, 2 stanzas of 6 and 4 lines, as published in *Poetry* (January 1933) and CP. Top center, "10" in pencil.

D80. "The Sad Indian". T.ms., 1p. (black ribbon). NNC

Title: THE SAD INDIAN

First line: Sad heart, the gymnast of inertia, does not count

Collation: 1 sheet of typing paper. 26.7 x 20.5 cm.

Contents: Typescript, 2 stanzas of 6 and 4 lines, as published in *Poetry* and CP. Top center, "10" in pencil. Typed lower right, "HART CRANE | (Copy)".

Note: Copy made by Samuel Loveman in 1932. NNC also has carbon copy of typescript.

D81. "The Sad Indian". T.ms., 1p. (black ribbon). ICU

Title: THE SAD INDIAN

First line: Sad heart, the gymnast of inertia, does not count

Collation: 1 sheet of typing paper. 25.5 x 20 cm.

Date: ca. 1930–1931.

Contents: Typescript, 2 stanzas of 6 and 4 lines, as published in *Poetry*. Editorial markings throughout.

D82. "Supplication to the Muses on a Trying Day". T.ms., 1p. (black ribbon). TxU

Title: SUPPLICATION TO THE MUSES ON A TRYING DAY

First line: Hold it in a high wind. The fender curving over the

Collation: 1 sheet of typing paper. 26.5 x 20.3 cm. Two holes punched along right margin.

Date: ca. 1930–1932.

Contents: Typescript of unpublished prose poem, 38 lines. Signed "Hart", lower right in ink.

D83. "They were there falling". T.ms., 1p. (black ribbon). NNC

First lines: They were there falling; | And they fell. And their habitat

Collation: 1 sheet of typing paper. 27 x 20.8 cm.

Date: ca. March-April 1932.

Contents: Typescript draft of unpublished poem, 16 lines, related to "The Circumstance"; corrections and emendations (Crane's hand in pencil). Top center, "18" in pencil.

D84. "This way where November takes the leaf". T.ms., 1p. (black ribbon). TNF

First line: This way where November takes the leaf.

Collation: 1 sheet of typing paper. 27.8 x 21.5 cm. (Enclosed in letter from Crane to Jean Toomer, 23 November 1923.)

Date: ca. 1923–1924.

Contents: Typescript draft of unpublished poem, 21 lines in 4 stanzas. Typed between stanzas 3 and 4, "(other verses even less developed- poem | ends with following lines:"; and typed at bottom of sheet: "I think I ought to apologize for this page as it stands! h".

D85. "To Conquer Variety". A.ms., 2p. (Crane's hand in pencil). NNC

Title: *To Conquer Variety*

First line: I have seen my ghost broken

Collation: 1 sheet of typing paper, written on both sides. 24.8 x 20 cm.

Date: ca. 1931–1932.

Contents: Handwritten draft of unpublished poem, 7 lines. Bottom left, "inexpugnable" in ink, and "Calendonia 1723" in red pencil (Crane's hand). On verso, miscellaneous notes relating to poem (Crane's hand in pencil).

D86. "To Earth". T.ms., 1p. (black ribbon). NNC

Title: To Earth

First line: Be earnest, Earth, - and kind.

Collation: 1 sheet of typing paper. 27.8 x 21.5 cm. (Enclosed in letter from Crane to the Rev. Mr. Charles C. Bubb, 13 November 1918.)

Date: ca. 1917–1918.

Contents: Typescript, 4 lines, as published in SL. Lower right, "Bubb A" encircled in pencil (unknown hand).

D87. "To Liberty". T. and a.ms., 1p. (black ribbon; Crane's hand in pencil). NNC

Title: T O LIBERTY

First line: Out of the seagull cries and wind

Collation: 1 sheet of tan typing paper. 27.7 x 21.3 cm.

Date: ca. 1927–1930.

Contents: Typescript and handwritten draft as published in BW, pp. 396–97. First 2 stanzas, 7 and 6 lines, in typescript, and final 7 lines in manuscript (Crane's hand in pencil).

D88. "To the Empress Josephine's Statue". A.ms., 1p. (Crane's hand in pencil). NNC

Title: *To the Statue*

Collation: 1 sheet of tan typing paper. 27.8 x 21.5 cm.

Date: ca. 1930–1932.

Contents: Handwritten notes, 11 lines (Crane's hand in pencil).

D89. "To the Empress Josephine's Statue". A.ms., 2p. (Crane's hand in ink). NNC

Title: To the Empress Josephine's Statue

First line: You, who contain, augmented tears, explosions

Collation: 1 sheet of typing paper, written on both sides. 27.5 x 21.3 cm.

Date: ca. 1930–1932.

Contents: Handwritten draft varying in several instances from version published in BW, p. 398. On recto, 15 lines, one notation in red pencil along left margin; on verso, 6 lines and several lines of notes (Crane's hand in ink).

D90. "To the Empress Josephine's Statue". T.ms., 1p. (black ribbon). NNC

Title: TO THE EMPRESS JOSEPHINE'S STATUE

First line: You who contain, augmented tears, explosions,

Collation: 1 sheet of typing paper. 26.5 x 20.3 cm.

Contents: Typescript, 2 stanzas of 12 and 9 lines, as published in BW, p. 398. Several notations in pencil (Samuel Loveman's hand). Typed lower right, "Hart Crane | (Copy)".

Note: Copy made by Samuel Loveman in 1932. NNC also has two carbon copies of typescript.

D91. "A Traveler Born". T.ms., 2p. (black ribbon). NNC

First line: Of those three sailors, and the silent main

Collation: 1 half-sheet of typing paper, written on both sides. 14 x 22.5 cm.

Date: ca. 1928–1930.

Contents: Early typescript draft, 5 lines, with 1 additional line in manuscript (Crane's hand in ink and pencil). At top of sheet is one typed line, "A home for serums, keeps its tubes involute", unrelated to poem. On verso title and the first 2 lines of later version typewritten.

D92. "A Traveler Born". T.ms., 1p. (black ribbon). NNC

First line: The sailors—those two Corsicans at Marseille,—

Collation: 1 half-sheet of typing paper. 14 x 22.5 cm.

Date: ca. 1928–1930.

Contents: Typewritten draft of 2 stanzas of 4 lines each; second last line canceled and 2 additional lines written beneath (Crane's hand in ink).

D93. "A Traveler Born". T.ms., 1p. (black ribbon). NNC

First line: Of sailors–those two Corsicans at Marseille–

Collation: 1 sheet of tan typing paper. 27.5 x 21.3 cm.

Date: ca. 1928–1930.

Contents: Typewritten draft of the first stanza, 4 lines, with 2 lines in manuscript beneath (Crane's hand in ink).

D94. "A Traveler Born". T.ms., 2p. (black ribbon). NNC

Title: A Traveller Born [Crane's hand in pencil]

First line: Of sailors–those two Corsicans at Marseille,–

Collation: 1 half-sheet of typing paper, written on both sides. 14 x 22.7 cm.

Date: ca. 1928–1930.

Contents: On recto, typewritten draft, 2 stanzas of 4 lines each, heavily corrected and emended (Crane's hand in ink and pencil). On verso, several drafts in pencil.

D95. "A Traveler Born". T.ms., 1p. (black ribbon). NNC

Title: A TRAVELLER BORN

First line: Of sailors–those two Corsicans at Marseille,–

Collation: 1 half-sheet of typing paper. 14 x 22.7 cm.

Date: ca. 1928–1930.

Contents: Late typewritten draft, 11 lines in 3 stanzas; corrections and emendations (Crane's hand in pencil and ink). Top center, "6" in pencil (probably Samuel Loveman's hand).

D96. "A Traveler Born". T.ms., 1p. (black ribbon). NNC

Title: A TRAVELER BORN

First line: Of sailors—those two Corsicans at Marseille,—

Collation: 1 sheet of typing paper. 26.5 x 20.3 cm.

Contents: Typescript, 2 stanzas of 4 and 5 lines, as published in *New Republic* (February 15, 1933) and CP; several notations (Samuel Loveman's hand in pencil). Typed lower right, "HART CRANE | (Copy)".

Note: Copy made by Samuel Loveman in 1932. NNC also has carbon copy of typescript.

D97. "The Visible the Untrue". T.ms., 1p. (black ribbon). NNC

First line: strohphe true of all my love

Collation: 1 sheet of typing paper. 27.8 x 21.5 cm.

Date: ca. 1930–1932.

Contents: Typewritten fragment related to final stanza, 5 lines.

D98. "The Visible the Untrue". T.ms., 1p. (black ribbon). NNC

Title: THE VISIBLE the UNTRUE [last word canceled and written again beneath in pencil, Crane's hand]

First lines: Yes, I being | the Terrible puppet of my dreams, shall

Collation: 1 sheet of typing paper, written on both sides. 27.8 x 21.5 cm.

Date: ca. 1930–1932.

Contents: Typewritten draft as published in *Poetry* (January 1933) and CP; corrections and emendations (Crane's hand in pencil). Title typed on verso.

D99. "The Visible the Untrue". T.ms., 1p. (black ribbon). NNC

Title: THE VISIBLE THE UNTRUE [third word written above in pencil, Samuel Loveman's hand]

First lines: Yes, I being | the terrible puppet of my dreams, shall

Collation: 1 sheet of typing paper. 26.5 x 20.5 cm.

Contents: Typescript, 4 stanzas of 8, 6, 4, and 5 lines, respectively, as published in *Poetry* (January 1933) and CP; notations (Samuel Loveman's hand in pencil). Typed lower right, "HART CRANE | (Copy)".

Note: Copy made by Samuel Loveman in 1932. NNC also has carbon copy of typescript.

D100. "The Visible the Untrue". T.ms., 1p. (black ribbon). ICU

Title: THE VISIBLE THE UNTRUE

First lines: Yes, I being | the terrible puppet of my dreams, shall

Collation: 1 sheet of typing paper. 25.5 x 20 cm.

Date: ca. 1930–1932.

Contents: Typescript as published in *Poetry* (January 1933). Editorial markings and notations throughout.

D101. "What miles I gather up and unto you". T.ms., 2p. (black ribbon). NNC

First line: What miles I gather up and unto you

Collation: 1 sheet of typing paper. 22.8 x 15.5 cm.

Date: April 1924 (see LHC, p. 183).

Contents: Typescript draft of sonnet, 15 lines, as published in BW, p. 395; sonnet later revised into "Voyages III" (see items A47 and A48). On verso, typescript draft related to "Voyages II".

D102."What miles I gather up and unto you". T.ms., 1p. (black ribbon). PU

Title: S O N N E T

First line: What miles I gather up and unto you

Collation: 1 sheet of typing paper. 28 x 21.5 cm.

Date: April 1924 (see LHC, p. 183).

Contents: Typescript draft of sonnet, 15 lines, as published in BW, p. 395; one emendation in ink (Crane's hand).

D103."What Nots?" T.ms., 1p. (black ribbon). OU

Title: WHAT NOTS?

First lines: What is a What Not | if what is not negates

Collation: 1 sheet of tan typing paper. 28 x 21.5 cm. (Enclosed in letter from Crane to Gorham B. Munson, 20 December 1923.)

Date: 20 December 1923.

Contents: Typescript of unpublished poem, 21 lines in 6 stanzas. Note on bottom of sheet (Crane's hand in pencil).

D104."With a Photograph to Zell, Now Bound for Spain". T.ms., 1p. (black ribbon). NNC

Title: WITH A PHOTOGRAPH | TO ZELL, NOW BOUND FOR SPAIN

First line: From Brooklyn Heights one sees the bay;

Collation: 1 sheet of typing paper. 27.5 x 21.4 cm. (Enclosed in letter from Crane to Grace Hart Crane and Elizabeth Hart, 21 October 1924.)

Date: 21 October 1924.

Contents: Typescript, 3 stanzas of 6, 8, and 6 lines, respectively, as published in *Columbia Library Columns* (May, 1966). Between title and text is pen-and-ink drawing by Crane of view of Brooklyn Bridge from window of his room.

D105. "You are that frail decision that devised". T.ms., 1p. (black ribbon). NNC

First line: You are that frail decision that devised

Collation: 1 half-sheet of ruled paper. 15.5 x 20.5 cm.

Date: ca. 1923–1926.

Contents: Typescript of unpublished fragment, 4 lines. Note by Samuel Loveman (in pencil) on bottom of sheet refers to typed note on verso signed "Ray".

E.

PROSE MANUSCRIPTS

E1. "From Haunts of Proserpine". T.ms., 3p. (black ribbon). ICU

Title: FROM HAUNTS OF PROSERPINE

Collation: 3 sheets of typing paper. 25 x 19.5 cm. Last two sheets numbered 2 and 3.

Date: ca. Winter 1931–1932.

Contents: Typescript of review of James Whaler's *Green River: A Poem for Rafinesque* (New York, 1931), as published in *Poetry* (April 1932) and BW, pp. 422–24. Editorial markings and notations throughout.

E2. "Note on the Paintings of David Siqueiros". T.ms., 2p. (black ribbon). NNC

Title: *NOTE ON THE PAINTINGS OF DAVID SIQUEIROS* [underlined in red ribbon]

Collation: 2 sheets of typing paper. 27.5 x 21.5 cm. Second sheet numbered 2.

Date: ca. October 1931.

Contents: Typescript of unpublished 420-word essay on Mexican painter David Siqueiros, whose portrait of Crane is reproduced as frontispiece to CP; corrections and emendations (Crane's hand in ink).

E3. "Note on the Paintings of David Siqueiros". T.ms., 2p. (black ribbon). ICarbS

Title: *NOTE ON THE PAINTINGS OF DAVID SIQUEIROS*

Collation: 2 sheets of typing paper. 27 x 20.8 cm. Second sheet numbered 2. Two holes pierced along left margin with gummed reinforcements.

Date: October 1931.

Contents: Typescript of unpublished essay on David Siqueiros. Typed on p. 2 lower right, "Hart Crane", and on lower left, "Mexico City, Oct.–'31".

E4. "Note on the Paintings of David Siqueiros". T.ms., 3p. (black ribbon). NNC

Title: *NOTE ON THE PAINTINGS OF DAVID SIQUEIROS*

Collation: 3 sheets of ruled notebook paper. 26.7 x 20.4 cm. Last two sheets numbered 2 and 3. Two punched holes along left margin with gummed reinforcements.

Date: October 1931.

Contents: Typescript of unpublished essay on David Siqueiros. Typed on p. 3 following text, left side, "Mexico City, Oct. '31", and on right side, "Hart Crane. | (Copy)".

E5. [Notebook of Accounts and Addresses] A.ms., 14p. (Crane's hand in ink and pencil). NNC

Title: Hart Crane's Notebook [in pencil on front cover, probably Samuel Loveman's hands]

Collation: Notebook of ruled paper with tan paper covers and strip of black cloth pasted along spine. "NOTE | BOOK" printed in black on front cover. 20.2 x 12.5 cm.

Date: 1925-1928.

Contents: First eight pages and final page of Notebook contain financial accounts in ink and pencil, dated December 1925 through June 1928, and five pages near the end contain names and addresses and brief notations. Major part of Notebook is blank.

E6. "A pure approach to any art . . . " T.ms., 1p. (black ribbon). NNC

First line: A pure approach to any art or creative endeavor . . .

Collation: 1 sheet of typing paper. 28 x 21.5 cm.

Date: ca. 1930.

Contents: Early typescript draft of 150-word essay on aesthetics.

E7. "A pure approach to any art . . . " T.ms., 1p. (black ribbon). NNC

First line: A pure approach to any art or creative endeavor . . .

Collation: 1 sheet of typing paper. 27.7 x 21.5 cm.

Date: ca. 1930.

Contents: Typescript of 250-word essay on aesthetics as published in BW, p. 424; emendations (Crane's hand in pencil).

E8. [Review of Howard Phelps Putnam's *The Five Seasons*] A. and t.ms., 7p. (Crane's hand in pencil; black ribbon). NNC

Note: In addition to manuscript fragments described below, there is another typescript draft of fragment of review on verso of manuscript of "Euclid Avenue" (see item D28).

Date: ca. October 1931–April 1932. (A copy of Howard
Phelps Putnam's *The Five Seasons* was sent to Crane
for review by the editor of *Poetry*, Morton Dauwen
Zabel, in October 1931 (see LHC, p. 384). Between
that time and his death, Crane worked on the review
but did not complete it. For Zabel's comments on Crane's
review see Zabel's own review of the book in *Poetry*,
vol. 40, pp. 335–36, September 1932.)

Contents:

a. [Notes] A.ms., 1p. (Crane's hand in pencil). 1 sheet
   of onionskin paper. 27.7 x 21.3 cm.

b. "Phelps Putnam's *The Five Seasons*". A.ms., 2p.
   (Crane's hand in pencil). 1 sheet of typing paper,
   written on both sides. 27.5 x 21.3 cm. Probably
   earliest draft of beginning portion of review. Typed
   upper left, "NOTE ON THE PAINTINGS OF
   DAVID SIQUEIROS", canceled in blue pencil.

c. "Acid Honor of the Sun". T.ms., 1p. (black ribbon).
   1 sheet of typing paper. 27.2 x 20.8 cm. Corrections
   and emendations (Crane's hand in ink and pencil).
   Draft of opening paragraph.

d. "In the Name of Chance". T.ms., 1p. (black ribbon).
   1 sheet of typing paper. 27.7 x 20.7 cm. Corrections
   in pencil (Crane's hand). Draft of two paragraphs,
   apparently intended to appear early in review.

e. Untitled draft of single paragraph apparently intended for central portion of review. T.ms., 1p. (black
   ribbon). 1 sheet of onionskin paper. 24.1 x 21.4 cm.
   Top part of sheet cut away. Several words canceled
   in pencil.

f. Untitled draft of two paragraphs apparently intended
   for central portion of review. T.ms., 1p. (black ribbon). 1 sheet of onionskin paper. 27.6 x 21.4 cm.
   Several words canceled in pencil. Expanded version
   of draft described under part "e".

g. Untitled draft of single paragraph apparently intended for central portion of review. T.ms., 1p. (black ribbon). 1 sheet of typing paper, with a rectangular portion cut out of bottom half of sheet. 26.5 x 20.2 cm. One correction in pencil (Crane's hand). Star drawn at bottom of sheet in blue and red pencil.

E9. "Title". A.ms., 2p. (Crane's hand in pencil and ink). NNC

Title: *Title* [Crane's hand in pencil]

First line: Pipe down, Pocohontas (name of comedy)

Collation: 1 sheet of typing paper, written on both sides. 25 x 20 cm.

Contents: Lists of humorous titles none of which were used in Crane's published writings; 2 lines in ink and 16 lines in pencil (Crane's hand).

E10. "Vocabulary". A.ms., 15p. (Crane's hand in ink and pencil). NNC

Title: Vocabulary [Crane's hand in ink, on white label with red border pasted on front cover]

Collation: Notebook with dark green paper covers. 12.6 x 6.8 cm.

Date: ca. 1923–1926.

Contents: Notebook of words, phrases, quotations, and miscellaneous names, addresses, and accounts (Crane's hand in ink and pencil). Central portions of notebook blank.

F.

CHECKLIST OF LETTERS
FROM HART CRANE

F1. *Anderson, Sherwood. 1 a.l.s., 1 t.l.s. Cleveland and n.p., 12 August 1920 and 10 January 1922. ICN

F2. Braithwaite, William Stanley. 1 t.l.s., 1p. Cleveland, 27 October 1922. MH

F3. Brown, Sue. 1 t.l.s., 1 t.l. (typescript copy). Woodstock and Isle of Pines, 13 November 1923 and 22 May 1926. NNC

F4. Brown, William Slater. 1 a.l.s., 2 p.c.s. V.p., 1925–1927. Collection of H. Bacon Collamore, Hartford

F5. Brown, William Slater. 3 t.l.s., 2 t.l., 4 t.l. (typescript copies). V.p., 1925–1930. NNC

F6. Brown, William Slater and Sue. 5 t.l.s., 3 t.l., 1 t.l. (typescript copy). V.p., 1925–1928. NNC

F7. Bryan, George B. 7 a.l.s., 11 t.l.s., 1 t.n., 2 p.c.s. New York and Cleveland, 1917–1919. OU

F8. Bubb, The Rev. Charles C. 1 t.l., 2p. (carbon copy). Cleveland, 13 November 1918. NNC

F9. Campbell, Roy. 1 t.l.s., 1p. Paris, 12 July 1929. ICarbS

F10. Cowley, Malcolm. 17 t.l. (typescript copies). V.p., 1923–1932. NjP

F11. Cowley, Malcolm and Peggy Baird. 3 a.l.s., 23 t.l.s., 5 t.l., 5 telegrams. V.p., 1923–1932. CtY

F12. Crane, Clarence Arthur. 2 t.l.s., 12 t.l. (carbon copies). V.p., 1910–1931. NNC

* Letters are arranged alphabetically by recipient.

F13. Crane, Clarence Arthur. 1 a.l.s., 23 t.l.s. V.p., 1917–1931. Collection of Norman Holmes Pearson, New Haven

F14. Crane, Grace Hart. 53 a.l.s., 99 t.l.s., 22 t.l. V.p., 1917–1927. NNC

F15. Crane, Grace Hart. 2 a.l.s. New York and Brooklyn, 9 January and 9 November 1924. OU

F16. Crane, Grace Hart. 1 t.l.s., 1p. Patterson, N. Y., 23 March 1926. TxU

F17. Crane, Grace Hart, and Elizabeth B. Hart. 5 a.l.s. Brooklyn, 1923–1925. TxU

F18. Crane, Grace Hart, and Elizabeth B. Hart. 1 t.l.s., 1p. Brooklyn, 21 October 1924. NNC

F19. Crosby, Caresse, 1 a.l.s., 1 t.l.s., 2 t.l. V.P., 1929–1932. NNC

F20. Crosby, Caresse. 7 a.l.s., 12 t.l.s., 2 telegrams, 4 cablegrams. V.p., 1929–1932. ICarbS

F21. Crosby, Harry. 5 a.l.s., 2 t.l.s., 2 t.l., 2 a.n.s., 1 p.c.s. V.p., n.d. and 1929. ICarbS

F22. Crosby, Harry and Caresse 2 a.l.s., 3 t.l.s., 1 p.c.s., 2 cablegrams. V.p., 13 March–31 October 1929. ICarbS

F23. *Dial,* Editors of. 27 t.l.s. V.p., 1923–1928. CtY

F24. Dietz, Lorna. 5 t.l.s., 2 p.c.s. V.p., 1930–1931. NNC

F25. Doherty, Mary. 1 t.l.s., 1p. Mixcoac, 20 April 1932. Files of John Simon Guggenheim Memorial Foundation, New York

F26. Frank, Waldo. 2 a.l.s., 37 t.l.s. V.p., 1923–1931. PU

F27. Grunberg, Solomon M. 2 a.l.s., 6 t.l.s., 1 t.l., 7 p.c.s. V.p., 1930–1932. NNC

F28. Hart, Elizabeth B. 5 a.l.s., 13 t.l.s., 1 t.l., 2 p.c.s. V.p., 1915–1927. NNC

F29. Hart, Elizabeth B. 1 a.l.s., 2p. Patterson, N. Y., 24 March 1926. NNC

F30. Hise, Bessie M. 8 t.l.s. V.p., 1931–1932. Collection of Norman Holmes Pearson, New Haven

F31. Hise, Bessie M. 10 t.l. (typescript copies). Mixcoac, 1931–1932. NNC

F32. Huebsch, Benjamin W. 2 t.l.s. (photocopies). Cleveland, 14 May and 27 June 1922. DLC

F33. Josephson, Matthew. 1 t.l. (p. 1 only). N.p. [October or November 1919?] CtY

F34. Kahn, Otto H. 2 a.l.s., 25 t.l.s., 1 t.l. V.p., 1925–1931. NjP

F35. Kahn, Otto H. 1 t.l.s., 6 t.l. (carbon copies) V.p., 1925–1927. NNC

F36. Laukhuff, Richard. 4 t.l.s. V.p., 1926–1932. ICarbS

F37. Loveman, Samuel. 1 a.l.s., 1 t.l.s., 1 p.c.s. V.p., 1926–1932. TxU

F38. Loveman, Samuel. 14 t.l.s., 1 a.n.s., 12 p.c.s. V.p. 1927–1932. NNC

F39. Mayfield, John S. 1 a.l.s., 1p. Patterson, N. Y., 6 November 1927. NSyU

F40. Moe, Henry Allen. 1 a.l.s., 7 t.l.s. V.p., 1930–1931. Files of John Simon Guggenheim Memorial Foundation, New York

F41. Monroe, Harriet. 2 t.l.s., 1 p.c.s. Brooklyn and n.p., 1930. ICU

F42. Munson, Gorham B. 44 a.l.s., 80 t.l.s., 4 p.c.s. V.p., 1919–1928. OU

F43. Munson, Gorham B. 1 t.l.s., 1p. Cleveland, 29 June 1921. ICarbS

F44. Rickword, Edgell. 1 t.l., 2p. (carbon copy). Patterson, N. Y., 7 January 1927. NNC

F45. Schneider, Isidor. 2 a.l.s., 8 t.l.s., 4 p.c.s. V.p., 1927–1932. NNC

F46. Schneider, Isidor and Helen. 2 a.l.s., 3 t.l.s. V.p., 1927–1930. NNC

F47. Selzer, Thomas. 1 t.l., 2p. (carbon copy). Brooklyn, 4 May 1925. NNC

F48. Simpson, Eyler N. 6 t.l.s. V.p., 1931–1932. Files of John Simon Guggenheim Memorial Foundation, New York

F49. Simpson, Mrs. T. W. 3 t.l.s., 2 p.c.s. V.p., 1926–1932. NNC

F50. Smith, Thomas R. 1 t.l.s., 1p. Mixcoac, 11 May 1931. NNC

F51. Stein, Gertrude. 1 a.l.s., 1 p.c.s. Paris and Collioure, 1929. CtY

F52. Stewart, Robert E. 1 t.l.s., 1p. Mixcoac, 3 April 1932. CtY

F53. Stieglitz, Mr. and Mrs. Alfred. 4 a.l.s., 7 t.l.s., 1 p.c.s. V.p., 1923–1929. CtY

F54. Tate, Allen. 8 a.l.s., 17 t.l.s., 3 t.l. V.p., 1922–1930. NjP

F55. Toomer, Jean. 3 a.l.s., 6 t.l.s., 1 t.l. V.p., 1923–1924. TNF

F56. Underwood, Wibur. 22 a.l.s., 1 a.n.s., 22 t.l.s., 4 t.l., 9 p.c.s. V.p., 1920–1932. CtY

F57. Untermeyer, Louis. 2 t.l.s. Chagrin Falls, Ohio, 18 and 24 July 1931. InU

F58. Vail, Lawrence. 1 p.c.s. N.p., n.d. NNC

F59. Van Doren, Irita. 1 a.l.s., 1p. Mixcoac, ca. 1931–1932. NNC

F60. Wiegand, Mr. and Mrs. Hermann von. 5 a.l.s., 9 t.l.s. V.p., 1919–1928. CtY

F61. Williams, William Carlos. 3 t.l.s. V.p., 16 September n.y. and 1923. NBuU

F62. Winters, Yvor. 1 t.l.s., 1p. New York, 1 November 1926. ViU

F63. Winters, Yvor. 1 t.l., 4p. (carbon copy). Patterson, N. Y., 29 May 1927. NNC

F64. Zabel, Morton Dauwen. 1 a.l.s., 10 t.l.s., 1 p.c.s. V.p., n.d. and 1931–1932. ICU

G.

CHECKLIST OF LETTERS
TO HART CRANE

G1. *Anderson, Margaret. 8 a.l.s. V.p., n.d. NNC

G2. Anderson, Sherwood. 18 a.l.s. V.p., 1919–1922. NNC

G3. Anderson, Sherwood. 19 a.l.s. and t.l.s. (carbon copies and photostats). V.p., 1919–1922. ICN

G4. Arden, Elsie. 1 t.l.s., 1p. N.p., n.d. NNC

G5. Brown, William Slater. 1 a.l.s., 1p. N.p., 11 October 1925. NNC

G6. Christensen, Pete. 1 a.l.s., 1 p.c.s. Oran, Algeria, and Riva, Italy, 12 April and 7 June 1930. NNC

G7. Clark, Ethel. 1 a.l.s., 3p. Chagrin Falls, Ohio, 6 December 1931. NNC

G8. Clarke, Florence. 1 t.l.s., 1p. New York, 8 May 1923. NNC

G9. Cowley, Malcolm. 1 a.l.s., 1 t.l.s., 1 p.c. V.p., 1923–1926. NNC

G10. Crane, Clarence Arthur. 35 t.l. (carbon copies). Cleveland, 1917–1931. Collection of Norman Holmes Pearson, New Haven

G11. Crane, Clarence Arthur. 1 a.l.s., 30 t.l.s., 4 t.l. (copies), 1 telegram. V.p., 1924–1931. NNC

G12. Crane, Grace Hart. 58 a.l.s., 1 a.n.s., 1 p.c.s., 11 telegrams. V.p., 1916–1930. NNC

G13. Crosby, Caresse. 7 a.l.s., 1 t.l.s. V.p., 1929-1930. NNC

* Letters are arranged alphabetically by sender.

G14. Crosby, Caresse. 2 t.l. (carbon copies). Paris, 17 February 1930 and 9 July 1931. ICarbS

G15. Crosby, Harry. 1 a.l.s., 8p. Paris, 1 March 1929. NNC (ICarbS has a photostat of this letter.)

G16. Crosby, Harry and Caresse. 1 a.l.s., 3p. [Paris] n.d. NNC

G17. Cummings, Anne Barton. 2 p.c.s. Silverlake, N. H., 6 and 23 June 1930. NNC

G18. Cummings, Edward Estlin. 1 a.l.s., 1p. Cambridge, Mass., 13 October 1927. NNC

G19. Curtis, Charles E. 1 t.l., 1p. Cleveland, 16 February 1926. NNC

G20. Deming, Zell Hart. 1 telegram. Warren, Ohio, 8 November 1928. NNC

G21. *Dial*, Editors of. 29 t.l. (carbon copies). New York, 1924–1928. CtY (These copies often appear on the versos of Crane's letters to *The Dial*.)

G22. Dimitrius, Mattoi. 1 p.c.s. Cargèse, Corsica, 29 May 1930. NNC

G23. Eliot, Thomas Stearns. 1 t.l.s., 1p. London, 16 August 1927. NNC

G24. Frank, Waldo. 7 a.l.s., 18 t.l.s., 1 p.c.s. V.p., 1922–1928. NNC

G25. Freeman, G. W. 1 t.l.s., 1p. New York, 19 August 1925. NNC

G26. Graves, Robert. 1 a.l.s., 2p. London, 25 March 1929. NNC

G27. Grunberg, Solomon M. 2 a.l.s. Baltimore, n.d. NNC

G28. Hart, Elizabeth B. 24 a.l.s. V.p., 1918–1927. NNC

G29. Hartley, Marsden. 1 a.l.s., 2p. Brooklyn, n.d. NNC

G30. Hise, Bessie M. 3 a.l.s., 7 t.l.s. V.p., 1931. NNC

G31. Huebsch, Benjamin W. 2 t.l.s. (photocopies). New York, 18 May and 7 August 1922. DLC

G32. Huebsch, Benjamin W. 1 a.l.s., 1p. New York, 25 February 1924. NNC

G33. Johnson, Oakley. 1 t.l.s., 1p. New York, 11 April 1932. NNC

G34. Jolas, Eugéne. 1 t.l.s., 2p. Paris, 24 February 1927. NNC

G35. Kahn, Otto H. 17 t.l.s. V.p., 1925–1930. NNC

G36. Kahn, Otto H., and secretary. 26 t.l., 1 telegram (carbon copies). V.p., 1925–1931. NjP

G37. Lachaise, Gaston. 2 a.l.s. New York, n.d. and 17 January 1927. NNC

G38. Lebègue, E. 1 p.c.s. Paris, 15 August 1920. NNC

G39. Madden, Bess. 1 t.l., 1p. N.p., n.d. NNC

G40. Madden, N. Byron. 1 a.l.s., 3 t.l.s. Cleveland, 17 Augus⸱ ⸱ 13 December 1931. NNC

G41. Mayfield, John S. 1 t.l.s., 1p. Austin, 31 October 192⸴ NNC

G42. Moe, Henry Allen. 1 t.l.s., 9 t.l. (carbon copies). Nev York, 1930–1931. Files of John Simon Guggenhein Memorial Foundation, New York

G43. Monroe, Harriet. 2 a.l.s., 1 t.l.s. Chicago, 1928–1931 NNC

G44. Moody, Harriet. 1 a.l.s., 1 t.l.s. Chicago, 23 March anc 2 July 1916. NNC

G45. Moore, Marianne. 3 t.l.s. New York, 28 October-27 November 1926. NNC

G46. Munson, Gorham B. 2 p.c.s. Rome and Florence, 7 and 15 February 1922. NNC

G47. Nagle, Edward. 1 a.l.s., 2p. Woodstock, N. Y., n.d. NN(

G48. O'Neill, Agnes. 1 t.l.s., 1p. Ridgefield, Conn., 31 October 1925. NNC

G49. O'Neill, Eugene. 1 a.l.s., 4 t.l.s. V.p., 1925–1926. NNC

G50. Oppenheim, James. 1 t.l.s., 1p. New York, 15 January 1932. NNC

G51. Pound, Ezra. 1 t.l.s., 1p. London, n.d. Collection of Norman Holmes Pearson, New Haven

G52. Rickword, Edgell. 3 t.l.s. London, 1926–1927. NNC

G53. Riding, Laura. 2 a.l.s., 1 p.c.s. V.p., 1926–1929. NNC

G54. Robson, Peggy Meras. 1 a.l.s., 8p. New York, 9 February 1932. NNC

G55. Rodman, Selden. 1 t.l.s., 1p. (last page only). N.p. [ca. October 1931] NNC

G56. Rosenfeld, Paul. 2 t.l.s. New York and York Harbor, Me., 18 September 1927 and 10 September 1929. NNC

G57. Saenz, Moises. 1 a.l.s., 4p. Mexico City, 13 August 1931. NNC

G58. Schneider, Helen. 1 t.l.s., 1p. New York, n.d. NNC

G59. Schneider, Isidor. 3 a.l.s. New York, n.d. NNC

G60. Schneider, Isidor and Helen. 1 a.l.s., 4p. [New York, Spring 1928] NNC

G61. Seaver, Edwin. 1 t.l.s., 2p. Woodstock, N. Y., 20 November 1924. NNC

G62. Simpson, Eyler N. 2 t.l. (carbon copies). Mexico City, 30 April 1931 and 10 February 1932. Files of John Simon Guggenheim Memorial Foundation, New York

G63. Simpson, Mrs. T. W. 31 a.l.s. Isle of Pines, 1925–1932. NNC

G64. Siqueiros, David A. 2 a.l.s. N.p. [ca. March 1932] NNC

G65. Smith, Harrison. 1 t.l.s., 1p. New York, 10 July 1925. NNC

G66. Sommer, William. 1 a.l.s., 1p. Cleveland, n.d. NNC

G67. Soupault, Philippe. 1 t.l.s., 1p. Paris, 15 February 1927. NNC

G68. Stein, Gertrude. 1 a.l.s., 1p. Paris, 3 November 1929. NNC

G69. Stieglitz, Alfred. 11 a.l.s. V.p., 1923–1927. NNC

G70. Stuart, Robert. 1 a.l.s., 2p. Guantanamo Bay, Cuba, 16 March 1930. NNC

G71. Tate, Allen. 6 a.l.s., 14 t.l.s., 1 t.l. V.p., 1922–1930. NNC

G72. Thompson, Robert. 1 p.c.s. Martiques, France, 9 June n.y. NNC

G73. Toomer, Jean. 2 t.l. (carbon copies). Ellenville, N. Y. and n.p., 30 September 1923 and ca. 7 June 1924. TNF

G74. Toomer, Jean. 1 a.l.s., 1p. Amenia, N. Y., 5 November 1928. NNC

G75. Tully, James. 1 a.l.s., 1p. New York, 30 April 1928. NNC

G76. Wiegand, Charmion Habicht von. 1 p.c.s. Bordeaux, 3 February 1922. NNC

G77. Williams, William Carlos. 1 a.l.s., 2p. Rutherford, N. J., 17 April 1917. NNC

G78. Wright, William. 2 t.l.s. Warren, Pa., and New York, 23 October n.y. and 29 March 1923. NNC

G79. Zabel, Morton Dauwen. 12 t.l.s. Chicago, 1931–1932. NNC

INDEXES

Index to Names and Titles

Index to Repositories and Collections